NO STONE LEFT UNTURNED

HOW TO CASH IN ON THIS HIDDEN TREASURE IN THE TAX CODE
(That Can Save You Hundreds of Thousands in Retirement)

DANIEL RONDBERG

Foreword by Tom Hegna and Van Mueller

Copyright and Disclaimer

This publication is designed to provide accurate and authoritative information with regard to the subject matter covered. It is sold with the understanding that the publisher is not engaged in rendering legal, accounting, or other professional advice. If legal advice or other expert assistance is required, the services of a competent professional should be sought.

The author wishes to acknowledge the respective sources for use of graphs, charts, and other data in this book, and it is the author's intent to portray that data accurately rather than through representations.

This book may contain technical or other errors. Daniel Rondberg and The Retirement Research Foundation do not guarantee its accuracy, completeness, or suitability. In no event shall Daniel Rondberg or The Retirement Research Foundation be liable for any special, indirect, or consequential damages relating to this material for any use of this material or for any referenced website and courses, or the application of any idea or strategy in this book.

The information contained in this book is provided by Daniel Rondberg and The Retirement Research Foundation, and it is offered for educational and informational purposes only. Daniel Rondberg is a licensed insurance agent. He suggests that you consult with a qualified legal or tax-planning professional with regard to your personal circumstances. Nothing in this book should be interpreted or construed as legal, regulatory, insurance, tax, or financial planning advice or as an offer to perform services related to any of these fields in any respect.

The content of this book contains general information and may not reflect current legal, tax, insurance, or regulatory developments and information, and it is not guaranteed to be correct, complete, or current. Daniel Rondberg and The Retirement Research Foundation makes no warranty, expressed or implied, as to the accuracy or reliability of this information or the information contained in any referenced website or course.

Readers of this book should not act or refrain from acting on the basis of any information included herein without seeking appropriate legal or other relevant advice related to the particular facts and circumstances at issue from an attorney or other advisor duly and properly licensed in the recipient's state of residence. Daniel Rondberg and The Retirement Research Foundation expressly disclaim all liability with respect to actions taken or not taken by the reader based on any or all of the information or other contents within this book or provided by Daniel directly. Any information sent to Daniel Rondberg or The Retirement Research Foundation via Internet, e-mail, or through any referenced website is not secure and is done so on a non-confidential basis.

Should the reader of this book seek a referral to any service provider, the person to whom such referral is made is solely responsible for assessing the knowledge, skill, or capabilities of such provider, and neither the author, presenter, nor The Retirement Research Foundation is responsible for the quality, integrity, performance, or any other aspect of any services ultimately provided by such provider or any damages, consequential or incidental, arising from the use of such provider. Any opinions expressed in the book are mine alone and mine based on the information publicly available to me in my interpretation of that information.

Dedications

To my wife, Jennifer, for limitless faith and unconditional love. I am still the luckiest man alive. Thank God I saw you and that you waited for me.

Special thanks to:

My daughters, Cassidy and Spencer, for always coming through when it counts. You are my drive to leave this world a little better than I found it. One of the reasons why I wrote this in the middle of the night, is I want to spend as much time with you as possible. I am so proud of you, and I love being your Daddy. I love you so much.

Mom and Dad, together, for always believing in me and giving me the opportunity to find my calling.

Dad, individually, it was you and me against the world from the beginning.

Mom, individually, for coming into my life and teaching me that a Mother can love.

Matthew, my brother, for being the other half of Dbo and Mman.

Madison, my sister, for being the sister I always wanted.

Karen, my mother-in-law, for welcoming me into your family and encouraging me every step of the way. Thank you for Jennifer.

Matt Swartz, for saving my life (and helping me write this book).

Luke Miller, for showing up right when I needed you.

Fran Rainey, for teaching me how to earn something.

Ashleigh Greifzu, for taking me under your wing. I would not be here without your generosity.

Donnie Thibodaux, for teaching me the principles of leadership and business.

Every client who gave me a shot when I was young and starting out. There are too many kind people to thank, but I truly love you all.

Van Mueller, for molding me into the professional I'm proud to be.

Tom Hegna, for your contribution to our society. It's an honor to have a true legend be a part of this with me.

Larry Kotlikoff, for your generosity and for providing the insightful interview for this book as only you can.

My Aunt Sue Ritchie, "The Baby Boomer Lady & Authority on the 2030 problem," for encouraging me to join this business and showing me the way.

My Aunt Jody and Uncle Steve Sather, for being an inspiration and opening their home to me to visit every year.

Dustin Lester from Progressive Financial Concepts and QLS, for your insightful interview that contributed tremendously.

Diane Alber, for mentoring me through my first book.

Mark Renberg from Renberg CPAs, for being a true strategist, trusted CPA, and friend. Also, for the tax analysis that went into this book.

Ken Starks from Allied First Bank, for going to bat for me when I needed you most.

Paul Christoffers, for your interview and contribution to this book.

Zachary Markham, Co-owner of Fidelis Consultants, for giving me an opportunity.

Paul Roshka, Craig Waugh, and TJ Mitchell of Polsinelli and David Childers of Kutak Rock, for being our guardian angels and to David individually for your review of this book.

Brian Taylor and Ben Skinner of Taylor Skinner Law, for taking care of so many of our clients.

Rich Bell, for always being there for me and reviewing the tax examples.

Kris, for traveling the world with me.

Mo Swailem, for believing in me and working for a year for free to help me build my business and sticking with me through the failures and successes.

Brian North, for believing in me from the beginning.

Ronald Essary from IPG, for stepping up and having our back.

Brian King from IPG, for teaching me the behind the scenes of the business.

Marjorie Allen, for facilitating everything in my business for my clients and being a great friend through trying times. I could not do what I do without you

Fronge Wilson, for becoming family over five years and putting up with me long enough to see me grow

Kat Young for being an amazing partner to work with and breathing new life into our business

Jessica Naney, for saving me more times than I can count and coming back to us when we needed you the most. Aren't you glad I typed this?

Heather Monica, for helping transform me from a beginner to an expert.

Eric Paliga, for mentoring me and allowing me to mentor you.

Lisa Williams Digital BGA, for getting me to number one, four years in a row!

Ashby Hall, for helping me stay the course and being a constant support.

Will Franco, for teaching me the power of video and getting my business off the ground

Tom Kestler, for taking the time to give me the keys to starting my own business without asking for anything in return

Jason Walter, for spending an enormous amount of time training me so I could get started in the business

Dawnyel Smink, President of Canyonlands Insurance, for becoming a fast friend and giving so much to this project!

Michael Blaker, one of my first mentors who taught me the magic of a process.

Christie Olivas, for believing in me and giving me my first opportunity in finance.

Finally, my namesake, the original Dan Rondberg, my grandfather, and his wife Lois Lee Rondberg, my grandma. I hope I bring honor to your name every day, Nanny and Poppy. I love you and miss you both.

Table of Contents

Foreword by Tom Hegna

Daniel Rondberg is a great storyteller. You will see that very soon. He shares real-world stories with you that show how the Life Insurance Industry was built for times like these! It's ironic, but it seems that people only listen to a message when life punches them in the face: a loved one dies or gets laid off, or the market crashes. The concepts and techniques that Daniel shares are well known by leaders in the insurance industry. Unfortunately, they are not well known by the public.

Why is that you may ask? Because many of the "talking heads" on TV have their own agendas and will tell you to "only buy Term Life Insurance." Or they suggest "Don't buy annuities." Or they say, "The stock market always goes up." Or they advise "Maximize your 401k contributions." None of this is correct for many Americans. In reality, the only policy that matters is the one that is in force on the day that you die. Fewer than 2% of Term policies are in force when someone dies. Term Life insurance will not provide you tax-free income in retirement, which is even more important now that the government has printed and handed out more money than ever. Remember, the government has NO money—it must come from you and me. Taxes will have to go precipitously in the future.

ONLY an annuity can guarantee you will never run out of money. Retirement has been studied by PhDs around the world who unanimously agree that Longevity Risk is the #1 risk in retirement; ONLY an annuity can protect you from that risk. Dr. Roger Ibottson studied Fixed Index Annuities vs. Bonds. He found that Fixed Index Annuities have outperformed bonds for the last 40 years, and they are likely to outperform them for the next 40 years as well. We have all seen that the stock market doesn't always go up. We have seen people who have said they don't panic, panic. People who said they wouldn't sell when the market goes down—

sell. The people who owned annuities had guarantees that allowed them to NOT panic and to NOT sell and, instead, to weather the storms.

Maximizing your 401k contributions is so 1980ish. Back then, tax rates were higher. It made perfect sense to have money taken out of your paycheck, get a tax deduction, let it grow tax-deferred, and then take it out when you are in a lower tax bracket during retirement. It made PERFECT sense. We all did it. But look at where we are now. The national debt will soon be $25 Trillion. Social Security, Medicare, Medicaid, military pensions, and government pensions are all underfunded by more than $200 Trillion. So, where do you think tax rates are going from here? This is not a political question; it is a MATH question. I can tell you there is a 100% chance that taxes MUST go up in the future.

So, how will that impact YOU and YOUR retirement? Well, that is what this book is about. You might be able to see your current 401k balance (or should I say 201k), but you have NO IDEA how much income that 401k will provide for your retirement. You don't know what interest rates will be. You don't know what tax rates will be (other than much higher than today). Does that sound like a solid retirement plan? Not for me. I have been using the techniques that Daniel shares in this book for myself and my family. When the markets crash 40% or 50%, it doesn't affect MY retirement. I don't want it to affect your retirement either.

There ARE solutions. They are hiding in plain sight. Allow Daniel to reveal these to you in this book. You can easily read this book in an hour or two. Listen to the stories. Read his source information. Do your own due diligence. I am confident you will find that he is correct. By making a few minor changes now, you can be positioned to weather the coming storms. Markets will crash again, taxes will go up, and people will continue to live longer. Make the right decisions, and you will be much happier in retirement than your neighbor. Research now shows you are likely to live longer as well. Great things happen when you make great decisions!

Foreword by Van Mueller

This book should be recommended reading for all Americans. The narrative provides information that is not readily available to the American people. It is vital that at a minimum, Americans have an awareness of this information if they wish to make successful choices for achieving financial and retirement success. The challenges we face in the future are overwhelming.

No Stone Left Unturned provides a discussion of various considerations for planning that include, but are not limited to, higher future healthcare costs, higher taxes, and increased inflation and volatility.

Longevity will be the most serious of these challenges. This book provides awareness and possible solutions that can be considered to successfully face all the challenges we will face in our future.

Strategies provide certainty. Not planning builds uncertainty. Reading this book will help to inspire a positive choice.

Van Mueller LUTCF, LACP

Preface

COVID-19

Sadly, as I sit here writing my book, our country is currently being torn apart by this horrible virus. It descended upon us quickly and had a sudden unbelievable impact on all our lives. My heart is with families around the world who are praying for their loved ones to recover. My mind is on businesses, both family-owned ones like mine and large corporations that employ other families. Your political view is not what I care to know about you during this time. All I care about is your heart and determination to beat this virus and stand together to take action against the fire rain that will continue to bear down upon us.

I wrote this book in an immediate response to the severe economic impact the Tax Reform will have on all our retirements. It is designed to be the tool that you need most during this time to learn about and evaluate the strategies you can use to position you and your family to pay the least tax at the time you need your retirement savings the most. Fortunately, fate would have it that I would complete this book in January 2019 and shelve it for the entire year to focus on executing the strategies during that time personally.

Then, suddenly one night in December of 2019, it would be put on my heart so strongly, and with such conviction, that in the middle of the night, I would continue to work around the clock until this very moment. Even though my wife and I just had our second daughter, I told her that I know I am supposed to be doing this right now. I had no idea it was to accelerate my process to get the message out now. I am not saying that I predicted in any way that we would be facing this. My conviction is based on the already overwhelming economic evidence and government reports that urge Americans to exercise their rights and seize what could be their final opportunity to position their taxable retirement accounts in the most favorable way possible before the national debt forces the government to find more revenue.

However, I had no idea that in March of 2020, the government would pass a stimulus bill to save the economy that would add approximately 10% to our already unsustainable debt in a single week. And, even more stimulus money may be required. What will happen when the government needs more money to bail out corporations that are deemed "Too Big To Fail" or private and even public pension funds?

If you've been financially harmed by COVID-19, just think about what will happen when the taxpayer is forced to pay the bill for all of this. I am not blaming the government for this. That's not my message. My message is one of hope in a time of uncertainty. More than ever before, the strategies described in this book will be statistically more important to understand and execute before the window of opportunity closes. If economists are correct, the window may not open again in your lifetime. Please stay safe and healthy, and allow my words to serve you through this time. We are all in this together.

> *The lifeboats of the RMS Titanic played a crucial role in the disaster of 14–15 April 1912. One of the ship's legacies was that she had 20 lifeboats that in total could only accommodate 1,178 people, despite the fact that there were approximately 2,208 on board. RMS Titanic had a maximum capacity of 3,547 passengers and crew.*

No Stone Left Unturned is a realization I had about a little-known provision in the tax code of Publication 525. It was such a profound realization that it changed my practice and the lives of many people I work with.

Financial institutions flew representatives out to my office in Mesa, Arizona to see what I'd been working on. Once they learned of this hidden provision and how to use it properly, they enlisted me to teach their insurance agents, financial advisors, CPAs, and attorneys around the country how they can also use what I argue is one of most significant provisions still left in the U.S. tax code.

While traveling the country, I learned that not one of these professionals understood what this publication was or how to use it. I knew it was my job to help as many people as I possibly could overcome what I believe is going be the most significant risk to retirement.

In this book, I will mathematically prove that the government will need revenue at some point, and one of the sources of revenue will likely be higher (much higher) taxes. Also, there is a significant mathematical probability (which increases every day) that you or your spouse will need extended health care or long-term care in your retirement that will, no doubt, be much more expensive than it is today.

If these two events (increased taxes and healthcare costs) occur simultaneously, it will be arguably the most significant risk that anybody could face in retirement. And it could end up destroying the retirement you set up today if you are not adequately prepared. It will be the iceberg to the great journey of your retirement's Titanic.

I wrote this book because I realized that I need to get this information out to as many people as I possibly can as fast as possible. This is a warning call on the dock of the Titanic. Think of it like iceberg insurance being sold a week before the voyage ever took place.

Publication 525 has a little-known provision that allows you to transfer the exact amount of tax-free wealth to yourself at the precise time that you need it. Also, I'm going to show you step-by-step how you can analyze your scenario to establish and take advantage of the IRS's greatest provision to make sure that your retirement is secure.

Publication 525 is one of the most powerful tax-free delivery systems still left in the tax code. It is outlined in two paragraphs in thousands and thousands of pages of documentation. Publication 525 is not only a map of the Atlantic with the exact location and size of every single iceberg, but it is like a fleet of submarines traveling far ahead, destroying every single iceberg in your path, allowing safe passage through the greatest and most dangerous journey of your life—your retirement.

So, unless you learn the significance of Publication 525 and how to leverage it, you might find your big beautiful 401(k) sticking halfway out of the frigid ice waters of a place you do not want to be. Think I'm too dramatic? Think you're prepared? This book contains reports that suggest more than 70% of retirement plans will fail because of this significant oversight. I've spoken to, and continue to speak to, thousands of financial professionals, and not a single one knew what Publication 525 was or realized its significance for their clients. So, that was my realization. It was time to write a book.

In this book, you will find the guide to understanding specific undervalued provisions of Publication 525 and details on using the tools for which it provides tax-free exceptions. This book could literally show you how to take hundreds of thousands of dollars currently earmarked for the IRS and redirect it back into the hands of you and your family. The most famous IRA expert, CPA, Ed Slott, says that this is the single greatest benefit of the tax code.

This book is not meant to be read once and then set aside. It is not a paperweight, dust collector, or fire starter, but it is intended to be a tool—a reference guide in which each chapter invokes thought, reflection, and conversations. It is designed for readers to go straight to a specific chapter and apply the contents to their individual situation.

No Stone Left Unturned refers to the theory I developed for my clients, where we don't recommend anything unless we feel confident that we've exhausted all viable opportunities to ensure that we've done our job to the best of our ability. It's this philosophy that led to this strategy and the need to write this book. Unless you're willing to look under every stone, you may be stuck with the traditional options when this newly-developed problem, which has now intensified due to recent economic and healthcare-related events, will require a new solution. However, this practice is for life insurance agents only—not to teach them how to sell, but to be a thought catalyst to get them to see themselves in a more important role in their community at one of the most important times in history.

It is my vision that every agent hears the message contained within this book and starts a conversation with someone in their community that could alter the course of both of their lives forever. Many people have tried to stop this conversation, but as you can tell from my dedication page, I've been blessed by the encouragement of many others. I have had many unique conversations after my live presentations, and I hope to speak to as many agents as I can to impact their communities!

The SECURE Act

The SECURE Act was signed into law December 20, 2019.

Let me just stop here. Does anyone else find it odd that all major laws that have subtle but drastic consequences for baby boomers (aka the government's most expensive problem right now) are all being signed into law a few days before Christmas???

Do you think anyone is really paying close of attention to new legislation on fiduciary offerings of annuities inside 401(k) plans that close to Christmas? Or, anytime for that matter.

Here is a list of the most recent massive changes to the law that literally will remove billions, and some project over time, trillions right out of the hands of baby boomers...

By the way before I get to the list, if all of this tax deferral worked so well then why do most Americans not have enough money for retirement?

Fifty percent of Americans have less than $25,000 at retirement. When the government needs the money, do you think they can go after that group to get it? Or, will they be targeting the group that has $250,000 in a tax deferred account like a 401(k), 403(b), IRA Annuity, etc.? These accounts might as well be a neatly wrapped Christmas presents underneath the IRS's tree come Christmas morning.

Many people ask, "Are they really going to raise taxes or take away tax free privileges? Will I be grandfathered in?" If the last decade has taught us anything, it's that the government doesn't come out and make big announcements or offer clear communication that they are taking more of your money.

Instead, they hide the practice inside of legislation that they pass during the least noticeable time, What's more is, they do it in the most stealthy of ways, slowly and over a period of years, to future generations who aren't currently impacted and don't understand the impacts of these changes.

They are taking our money by the fistful in plain sight while staring into our eyes and we can't see it.

Let me give you an example: Do you think the average 50-year-old who has never received a single Social Security check or paid one Medicare premium has a clue or even cares what the government is doing with sequestration involving the Medicare trust or the restricted application with Social Security?

I surveyed my course participants after The SECURE Act. Here's what I found:

Before I informed them,

- Ninety percent did not know that The SECURE Act included provisions that impacted their retirement.

- Seventy-five percent did not know it was even being brought to the senate as a bill.

- Thirty percent did not know it passed at all.

- And 96% could not tell me one thing about it.

If you don't think the government understands this data and is using it to their advantage, then, sadly you will never be able to use the same data to take advantage of it.

I am not a conspiracy theorist, despite how what I have written will be perceived. We still live better than 90% of the planet.

I believe that this is the greatest country in the world. I love my America because I have freedom, and one of those freedoms is to use my voice to express my thoughts and speech. So, let me be clear with my message: Take advantage of this current era of economic growth and low taxes because if you don't, the rest of your life may be spent in a lifeboat staring down at the water wishing you could go back and save your vessel. Head boldly into the greatest voyage of your life and take this preparation seriously as I believe it will be one of the most important provisions you can embrace to enjoy your happily ever after.

Top Changes Since the SECURE Act of 2019

- Required Minimum Distribution (RMD) increased until age until 72.

- Annuities are now offered inside 401(k) plans.

- The inherited or stretch IRAs for spouses have been shortened to no more than a duration of ten years.

The law included many other significant changes to retirement accounts and tax credits; however, a simple file search will provide you with further details. While this will not impact all retirees, for those who are impacted, there will be significantly higher taxes to beneficiaries. It's like the old estate tax law jokes. When the estate tax was much lower, it was hard for a guy to be sitting around at the bar complaining that he wrote a check for $1,000,000 to the IRS because that means he also inherited $1,000,000. Nobody is feeling sorry for that guy, but that's not the issue. This issue is his hard working parents just gave half their life savings to an organization who will waste it by the time you finish reading this sentence.

Sadly, many other families who worked their entire lives will do the same. And while a few million dollars is literally nothing to our government, it could mean education, business funding, first homes, weddings, charitable donations, and financial freedom for that hard-working family for generations. So, I encourage you to take advantage of the tools in this book to appropriately determine if there are any areas of your situation where these tools are applicable. It really just comes down to this last question, would you rather give your hard-earned money to the government, or to yourself and your family? Thank you again for reading my life's work.

Introduction

No Stone Left Unturned refers to how I operate for my clients. I first heard Arnold Schwarzenegger use this term when describing how he did anything that it took and looked for any opportunity to reach his goal of being named Mr. Olympia. *No Stone Left Unturned* is how I approach looking for solutions for people who trust me. I feel an enormous amount of responsibility to provide as much knowledge and resources as I possibly can to help my clients or prospects in any way possible. Nothing fills me with more joy than seeing how others are excited to learn new ways to achieve their dreams as they furiously take notes in our meetings.

If you were given this book by someone close to you, someone you trust, know that they looked under many stones to find the right tool to help you retire confidently.

I believe *No Stone Left Unturned* is best read when it's a proactive message and the reader has time to receive the information in the best frame of mind and emotional state. This book is not meant to be read in a panicked state. Often when I study historical events like the Titanic, for example, my heart always goes to the moments after the boat began to sink and the anxiety of trying to save the passengers was rampant. I think of those gut-wrenching scenes from the movie when women are trying to throw their babies into lifeboats and people are jumping into the icy dark waters.

This book, if read ahead of the tragedy, would be like a letter to the captain of the Titanic containing a map with the geographical location of each iceberg in the Atlantic, a coupon for 100 more life boats, adequate disclosures that must be read to the passengers, hot air balloons on deck, and a fleet of submarines that would travel ahead of the ship in a protective wedge. Does your retirement have that level of protection? Do you think that level of safety is over-kill? Well, the passengers of the Titanic probably would have appreciated the owners looking under a few more stones.

The economic concepts and strategies discussed in this book are not the traditional stones you've already examined and put back down. There will be new and innovative information described in a way that you've never seen before. I can say that confidently (not arrogantly) because I have traveled the country discussing these concepts and found less than 10% of my audience of all financial professionals were aware of the topic. I created examples by doing the math behind some historical events and legislation that I've never been able to find in my research. My hope is that this is something new and this is that last stone that catches your eye. You think, "I probably don't need to pick it up," but something inside of you draws you over to it; it's just what you were looking for because there is treasure underneath.

The phrase *Leave No Stone Unturned* means "to do everything you can to achieve a good result, especially when looking for something." It originated in the mid-1500s in an ancient Greek legend about a general who buried his large treasure after being defeated. Those searching for the treasure consulted the Oracle of Delphi, who advised them to look under every stone.

The thing I hear most often when I sit down with a new client is, "I wish I had met you ten years ago." This book forecasts the most significant future risk to your retirement that you can prevent today if you understand and properly use the tools described by Publication 525.

Around the time tax reform had already crested the horizon and was bearing down upon us, I developed a conversation that I now have with my personal clients. The goal was simple—to leverage this tremendous economic opportunity to secure a guaranteed safety net in retirement so that it doesn't have to come down to hoping there are enough lifeboats. None of my clients are leaving their retirement to mere hope. My clients know with certainty that we are working together so that when the day comes that our government can no longer mathematically keep their promises, my clients will be protected.

When can you get started? You already have just by reading this book to learn about the most undervalued provision of the tax code. When I realized how powerful this message really was, I packaged it up and took it around this great nation to every financial professional who would listen. I shared my knowledge with them in the desperate hopes that they would carry the message to their clients, and we could help as many people as possible while there is still time.

How did we do it? I teach a class on tax reform all over the country, and when I train financial advisors and insurance agents, they say things like, "Well, Daniel, it's your energy. It's your passion. It's you. You're a talented young man."

And I say, "Well, you're right. If it's my passion, then get passionate. You know why I'm passionate? Because I read the reports. I read the materials saying that the government will not have enough money one day, and what do you think is going to happen when that day comes? Do you think they are going to let people go without their benefits, or do you think they are going to raise taxes? Are we okay with allowing Americans to sail into retirement by the boat full, believing they are passing all of their future income and net worth to themselves when we know there is going to be a scenario where the government is going to come for that money?"

The reports are screaming warning signs and people are being told to prepare. Tax reform gave us an opportunity to diversify. As a society, we have not only allowed people, but instructed them to sail into the unknown with all their cargo on a tax-deferred manifest where expensive tax collectors are waiting for them on the shore of their destination.

This could prove to be one of the most devastatingly bad pieces of advice uttered out of the mouths of our trusted financial professionals. Now, it has become our job to help them prepare for what's going to come.

If people only need a small income from their pre-tax money, they'll probably be fine (depending on their individual situation), but what if they need those dollars to help take care of themselves in retirement? What if they need long-term care? What is that going to look like? Their vessel will get crushed! The government could take 20%, 30%, or even 40% of that money back, and that will destroy any returns you had in your accounts. If the government takes 40%, it will be catastrophic. We need to help people prepare, and we need to do it right now! We need to do a heck of a better job making sure we are taking care of people.

In my travels, I've learned that most Americans (right now, the Baby Boomers) are heading into a retirement crisis that looks like this:

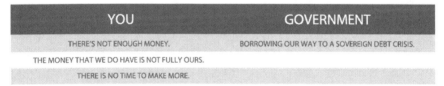

YOU	GOVERNMENT
THERE'S NOT ENOUGH MONEY.	BORROWING OUR WAY TO A SOVEREIGN DEBT CRISIS.
THE MONEY THAT WE DO HAVE IS NOT FULLY OURS.	
THERE IS NO TIME TO MAKE MORE.	

For most of us, retirement is a journey. Hopefully, it's the greatest journey we'll ever take. If retirement is the journey, your portfolio is the vessel that will make the great voyage. Although you're sailing into your golden years and the greatest destination of your life, you must use that vessel to travel through the freezing, shark-infested waters of our economy and other perils that are the risks to your retirement. Much like the great voyage of the Titanic, sadly, there will be icebergs.

Consider this your warning before your ship ever leaves the dock, not the warning that Frederick Fleet yelled when it was already too late. Think of it as iceberg insurance sold right at the dock before you ever get on board. This warning says yes, there are icebergs, and they are much like the iceberg that brought down the great Titanic, one of the largest vessels built during its time. You know that this risk exists. For many of you, it's a fleeting concern that you've thought of briefly like the tip of the iceberg sticking out of the ocean. But most of you will be unprepared to deal with the devastating effects of what lies beneath the surface. For many of you, this will sadly sink your vessel and end the once-fun ride, leaving you just trying to survive.

I'm not telling you not to take the journey. I'm only trying to warn you and to help you prepare so you don't need to worry about whether you have a lifeboat. By taking a small portion of your vessel and dedicating it to a special precautionary plan, we can show you how to add a guarantee to your voyage.

Think of it like having a hot air balloon on board instead of a lifeboat. You could deploy the exact solution at the exact time you need it to safely carry you and your family throughout the remainder of your journey and bravely navigate troubled waters when they hit. Sadly, the iceberg can't be avoided, but you and your family will be guaranteed safe passage throughout the rest of your journey up in the sky far above the dark waters in the clouds where tax-free heaven exists. How is that for a metaphor?

Nothing you're going to read in this book is my opinion nor is it exaggerated. Everything I'm going to share with you is based on facts that will prove the iceberg exists and how it can be avoided (or depending on what stage of life you're in, at least, survived) while there is still time to do something about it. I will provide examples and illustrations of hypothetical potential future tax environments. Remember, no one knows what the future holds. I will do my best to give some framework for these possible future scenarios in Chapter Two. Unfortunately, many Americans won't worry about how these scenarios affect their retirement accounts until it is too late.

I don't have any unique insider insights or access to anything that anybody else has. I just read—a lot. And, what I've read is disturbing; it has opened my eyes and has shown me that the government is steering us on a course with significant risks. Whether you believe it or not, it's just math.

Here is the problem:

This is your last chance to prepare. Are you confident your current strategy will work?

I'm not a conspiracy theorist. I'm not an anti-government person. I'm not an end-of-the-world doomsayer. I'm a concerned author in Phoenix, Arizona, who wants to get my message out. I didn't think I'd write this book; all I wanted was to help my clients. I didn't really have the time to put this together. So, why did I write a book? Why did I make the time? I wrote 99% of these pages between the hours of 1:00 am and 4:00 am because the message is that important. I'll sleep when I know the message is out there. I'll sleep when I know enough Americans acknowledge what's going to happen to their retirement accounts and take action to do something about it! Until then, I can't sleep.

There is an iceberg that is off in the distance, and we are rapidly approaching it. We have no idea what is beneath the surface, but we know it lies ahead. I'm going to prove it to you. Plus, I'll show you what can be done about it while there is still time. I am going to share with you the provision of the income tax code that can make the difference between success and failure.

Chapter One: The Problem

"Having tax diversification gives me options to manipulate the tax code to my advantage, rather than be manipulated by it."
– Jeff Bush, Nationally recognized political and tax thought leader

"You should be urging every single client to diversify their taxes while they're historically low."
– Tom Hegna, Economist, 2018 economic commentary

"A clever person solves a problem. A wise person avoids it."
– Albert Einstein

Fear paralyzed my body. The words of the speaker in front of me became muffled until they were drowned out by my anxiety, and I heard nothing. He was only a 45-year veteran in the financial services industry and the CEO of the company putting on this training summit. My palms were wet and cold, my stomach was weightless, my mind raced, and I heard the inner monologue take over, "Just pretend everyone is in their underwear."

As I tried visualizing this, another voice interrupted my failed image, "That is stupid. Just focus on your message and speak from your heart."

Sitting on the side of the stage, I felt the pressure rise like the tide until the tension was level with my shoulders. I couldn't breathe. How the heck was I going to speak? I glanced at the clock as it painfully narrowed within two minutes of my time to take the stage.

Just then, I heard a real voice. "Hey Daniel, you're almost up. Are you ready? They are falling asleep out there. It's all up to you."

I snapped back to reality, and suddenly the CEO's voice was crystal clear, "And this next young man, I've had the privilege of ..."

"Yeah, I'm ready to rock and roll," I said without turning my head to acknowledge the voice behind me.

I don't know if you're terrified of public speaking like I was but lying like this to psyche yourself up is common practice.

As the clock hit 11:00 am, one last thought popped into my head.

"If you knew you were going to die the second you walked off this stage, what would you want your final message to be for these advisors to carry on and echo to their clients and the families that rely on them?"

Boom! The adrenaline took over. I went to 120% instantly! The fear flushed out, and the megawatts of pure passion seized my every muscle. My confidence was being driven by the fact that I was ready. I've lived and practiced this for six years, and now it is my first opportunity to expand my reach. I can deliver my message to these 150 advisors so that, hopefully, they carry out this training with their clients, and I can reach thousands of households.

The voice on the microphone blared back into clarity.

"Please welcome your keynote speaker, Daniel Rondberg!"

I took the stage to the applause, and I have never looked back.

I'm Daniel Rondberg, and I teach a class with a curriculum that I wrote to train insurance agents, tax professionals, and financial advisors all over the country. I'm 30 years old. How did I get here so fast? When the Tax Cuts and Jobs Act was passed on December 19, 2017, I decided to triple-down in an area of our practice that I had been focused on since I joined the independent Arizona-based Nation's First Financial agency. Before you decide I'm too young to know anything, here is a list of people much younger than me who helped change the world:

- Alexander the Great founded his first colony at age 16.

- Augustus Caesar (Octavian) became a Roman Senator at 20.

- Joan of Arc turned a war around at 17.

- Wolfgang Amadeus Mozart wrote his first symphony at 8.

- James Madison joined the Continental Congress at 29.

- Mary Shelley published *Frankenstein* at 20.

- Ida B. Wells fought segregation at 27.

- Bob Woodward and Carl Bernstein exposed the Watergate scandal at 29 and 28.

- Malala Yousafzai won the Nobel Peace Prize at 17.

- Bobby Fischer was a Chess Grand Master at 15.

- John Lennon was age 17 and Paul McCartney was age 15 when they formed The Beatles.

- And the list goes on…

These people are extraordinary company, but my mission in writing this book for you is not to be on a list. It's to potentially help save your retirement. We need to start having a very important conversation about future events that will transpire for the average retirementsaver. I can't see into the future, but I can read data and, in doing so, I can predict the following:

1. The high probability of the government needing money is backed up by math and science.

2. It is likely you will live to the age of disability.

The combination of these two events occurring simultaneously is the problem, and it suggests, with almost 100% certainty, that the average retiree's savings plan will fail. Let me explain.

The reason the average plan will fail is that if all your retirement savings are in a fully-taxable account and the government raises taxes because they need revenue, it could cost you more to pull that money out for health care or long-term care and you could run out of money.

I've traveled the country having this conversation with thousands of CPAs, executives, attorneys, doctors, economists, financial advisors, and insurance agents. Do you know what I learned? No one is having this conversation, and I can say this with almost absolute certainty because I pioneered it. The combination of these two retirement risks occurring simultaneously has created a new, more serious threat, and, both have a high probability of occurring and are almost neck and neck in a race to see which one will occur first: future higher taxes and or future higher costs for quality extended care. If you plan to use your tax-deferred savings or physical assets to fund this, then your current plan may be set up to instead pay tremendous amounts of money to the government, nursing homes, and hospitals, and not to you and your family.

In my travels speaking and working in different professional practices, I've learned two things about the culture of retirement in our country:

1. The vast majority of investors save the bulk of their life savings in qualified plans (e.g., 401(k)s, IRAs, 457s, etc.).

2. Advisors rarely discuss a good exit plan for these accounts should a catastrophic healthcare event occur at some point over the course of retirement.

Here is where it gets scary. I'm going to share with you excerpts from my hour-and-a-half long, bone-chilling exclusive interview with Professor Laurence Kotlikoff of Boston University Department of Economics. In case you are unfamiliar with his work, here is a sample of his resume:

Laurence J. Kotlikoff is a William Fairfield Warren Professor at Boston University, a Professor of Economics at Boston University, a Fellow of the American Academy of Arts and Sciences, a Fellow of the Econometric Society, a Research Associate of the National Bureau of Economic Research, Head of International Department for Fiscal Sustainability Studies at the Gaidar Institute, President of Economic Security Planning Incorporated (a company specializing in financial planning software), and the Director of the Fiscal Analysis Center.

Professor Kotlikoff is a New York Times bestselling author and an active columnist. His columns and blogs have appeared in *The New York Times, The Wall Street Journal, The Financial Times, The Boston Globe, Bloomberg, Forbes, Vox, The Economist,* Yahoo.com, *Huffington Post,* and many other major publications. Also, he is a frequent guest on major television and radio stations. In 2014, he was named by *The Economist* as one of the world's 25 most influential economists. In 2015, he was named one of the 50 most influential people in Aging by Next Avenue.

Professor Kotlikoff received his B.A. in Economics from the University of Pennsylvania in 1973 and his Ph.D. in Economics from Harvard University in 1977. From 1977 to 1983, he served on the faculties of economics of the University of California, Los Angeles and Yale University. In 1981 and 1982, Professor Kotlikoff was a Senior Economist with the President's Council of Economic Advisers.

Professor Kotlikoff is the author or co-author of 19 books and hundreds of professional journal articles. His most recent book, *Get What's Yours: The Secrets of Maxing Out Your Social Security Benefits* (co-authored with Philip Moeller and Paul Solman, Simon & Schuster), is a runaway New York Times Bestseller.

Professor Kotlikoff has served as a consultant to the International Monetary Fund, the World Bank, the Harvard Institute for International Development, the Organization for Economic Cooperation and Development, the Swedish Ministry of Finance, the Norwegian Ministry of Finance, the Bank of Italy, the Bank of Japan, the Bank of England, the Government of Russia, the Government of Ukraine, the Government of Bolivia, the Government of Bulgaria, the Treasury of New Zealand, the Office of Management and Budget, the U.S. Department of Education, the U.S. Department of Labor, the Joint Committee on Taxation, the Commonwealth of Massachusetts, the American Council of Life Insurance, Merrill Lynch, Fidelity Investments, AT&T, AON Corporation, and other major U.S. corporations.

He has provided expert testimony on numerous occasions to committees of Congress, including the Senate Finance Committee, the House Ways and Means Committee, and the Joint Economic Committee.

I recommend you *Google* Professor Kotlikoff to fully appreciate his understanding of our country's fiscal state. His work freaked me out so much that I wasn't happy he confirmed my philosophies. The retirement crisis that we are on the cusp of is almost as severe as the moment Frederick Fleet spotted the iceberg on the Titanic and yelled, "Iceberg, right ahead!" In this book, I will reveal excerpts of the interview I conducted with Professor Kotlikoff where he warned that the U.S. is on the verge of a sovereign debt crisis.

To translate that from an economist definition, a sovereign debt crisis is what happened to Venezuela and Greece. The currency of a country becomes worthless, and people can no longer feed their families—so they riot and revolt. It's happened countless times throughout the world's history. In economists' terms, we will face austerity measures, which are official actions taken by the government during a period of adverse economic conditions to reduce its budget deficit using a combination of spending cuts or tax increases.

Using math and economic data, I'm going to prove to you that it is a matter of *when*, not *if*, this becomes a crisis. But don't jump overboard. Stay with me. Don't panic; just read on. I will show you the exact blueprint you can use now, today, to take corrective action and at least guarantee that you and your family will be in control of what will happen. We will explore the hidden power of Publication 525, the solution the IRS still allows under the current tax code. To do that, I'm going to bring you into the private conference room where I have personalized conversations with the people I have the privilege of serving every day. This will allow me to demonstrate how the average retirement saver is currently positioned and uncover the solution that will help them to fortify that position.

Key Takeaways from CHAPTER ONE: THE PROBLEM

- Start with this conversation. Share this conversation. Save your retirement with this message.

- The math and science behind the probability that the government will need money is very high.

- It is likely you will live to the age of disability.

- The average retiree's savings plan will fail because:

  o The vast majority of investors save the bulk of their life savings in qualified plans (e.g., 401(k)s, IRAs, 457s, etc.).

  o Advisors rarely discuss a good exit plan for these accounts should a catastrophic healthcare event occur at some point over the course of their retirement.

- The combination of these two events occurring simultaneously is the problem.

- Skip to *Chapter Six: The Interview* for the bone-chilling, hour-and-a-half long exclusive interview with Professor Laurence Kotlikoff, Boston University Department of Economics.

- Publication 525 contains the provision that will assist with the problem:

  o There's not enough money.

  o The money that we do have is not fully ours.

  o There is no time to make more money.

- o The government is borrowing our way to a Sovereign Debt Crisis.

- The reason the average plan will fail is that if all of your retirement savings are in a fully-taxable account and the government raises taxes because they need revenue, it could cost you more to pull that money out for health care or long-term care and you could run out of money.

- The combination of these two retirement risks occurring simultaneously has created a new, more serious threat, and both have a high probability of occurring and are almost neck and neck in a race to see which one will occur first—future higher taxes or future higher costs for quality extended care. If you plan to use your tax-deferred savings or physical assets to fund this, then your current plan may be set up to instead pay tremendous amounts of money to the government, nursing homes, and hospitals and not to you and your family.

Chapter Two: The Conversation

"We cannot solve our problems with the same level of thinking that created them."
—Albert Einstein

"I did then what I knew how to do. Now that I know better, I do better."
—Maya Angelou

"The past has no power over the present moment."
—Eckhart Tolle

"What do you think of the joke?" I asked my wife eagerly as she sat on the bed of our hotel room while I nervously paced the floor.

"That was a joke?" she asked, looking down at our daughter sleeping on our bed. That's never what you want your audience to say after telling a joke.

At least my family flew to Denver with me. It was the night before my keynote, and I was clutching my notes, hoping to potentially squeeze a joke out.

Historically, I have a bad track record when it comes to landing my jokes during these lectures. I can't tell you how many times I've heard crickets after a joke that I thought would kill. It's not that easy to lighten up these presentations, especially with this topic, but here it goes anyway.

Let me take you into my practice, into the very conversations I have with my clients to outline what could happen, to determine if you think this is important to plan for. This journey started for me in November of 2017 when I read the AARP article titled, "Senate Tax Bill Would Trigger Medicare Cuts."

(https://www.aarp.org/politics-society/advocacy/info-2017/
senate-tax-medicare-cuts-fd.html)

I'm going to share the transcript from one of my sample meetings with you, but let's have an interactive conversation through
the dialogue of this chapter. I'm going to use a client example, but
you can pencil in your own numbers in the margins to determine
your outcome. This is the conversation you have *not* had with your
current team of professionals.

Daniel: "I want to take a minute to share this article with you."

My Beloved Client: "Okay."

Daniel: "I feel like you want me to proactively bring things to
your attention and make you aware of them before they happen.
In working together, I feel like it's my job to say, "Hey, these are
the kinds of things we want to be mindful of in retirement." Do
you agree that you want me to be focused on those things?

My Beloved Client: "Yes, of course."

Daniel: "I never want there to be a scenario where you're sitting
across the table from me, and you look at me and say, 'Daniel, why
didn't you tell me about this before it happened?' That's my job,
right?

I read this article the other day, and my heart sank. I thought of
you, and I thought of all my clients, friends, and family. I want to
take a minute to discuss it because I think it's going to have a big
impact on all my clients who take Medicare benefits—you plan to
take Medicare as part of your retirement. What this article says is,

"Senate Tax Bill Will Trigger Medicare Cuts." Are you up to date on what's going on with the tax reform?

My Beloved Client: "No."

Daniel: "That's okay. There's a lot happening, but when I saw this article come up on my screen the other day (I take a minute to read the news every morning), it really caught my attention. I immediately Googled this article to fact-check what I was reading. What I found was that it was published by almost every major news outlet. It wasn't some small story that some news media place was trying to break for the first time. I eventually found AARP's article. Do you follow AARP?"

My Beloved Client: "Yes, I do."

Daniel: "They have good information. I follow it because they put out relevant topics for my clients to pay attention to. I read this article, and I have summarized what they're saying about this tax cut. The main point of the article is *Medicare is one of the only entitlements that the government can touch.* I didn't know that; I didn't think they could touch the entitlements. I thought you were entitled to your Social Security benefits, Medicare and Medicaid. But this tax reform does state that the government can start taking $25 billion out of the budget for Medicare… every… single… year. That's 4% (the max they're allowed to take). The government is going to go take 4% for the next ten years, which will drain the Medicare trust by 40%. So, if they take 40% of the budget out for Medicare, do you think healthcare is going to be less expensive in your retirement or more expensive?"

My Beloved Client: "More. "

Daniel: "Exactly. So, what are we going to do to make sure that doesn't happen to you? I want to share an interesting website with you called usdebtclock.org. Have you ever seen this site?"

My Beloved Client: "I have heard about it, but no, I haven't seen it."

Daniel: "Okay. This is important to me, and this is very interesting. This sites shows the national debt and how much is being spent every single second. (It's the debt clock, right?) Now, let's look at the three largest budget items in this national debt: Medicare and Medicaid, Social Security, and Defense and War. Medicare is the largest budget item. When you factor in the unfunded liabilities (the promises they've made to pay Americans), the national debt almost quadruples to $70 trillion!
Does it look like they can afford to take 40% more out of that budget?"

My Beloved Client: "No."

Daniel: "So, are doctors, hospitals, and pharmaceutical companies going to accept less money? Isn't that why we're in this position in the first place? Isn't that why when you go to the emergency room, you are charged $400 for an aspirin?"

My Beloved Client: "Right."

Daniel: "Doesn't that sound like a mess?"

My Beloved Client: "Yes, it does."

Daniel: "So, my point is, maybe it would be wise to plan and prepare for this. Here's the risk in this. Here's where I see why this is important for you and why I want to talk about it. We just did a review of all the annuities and IRAs I take care of for you. Let's pretend for a second that you have a catastrophic illness in your retirement; maybe you have a heart attack, stroke, or cancer, and now you need $100,000 for a procedure. You want to work with your skilled, trusted specialist, and they don't accept Medicare benefits anymore because right here, it says in the article, *Don't expect higher premiums right away. Don't expect higher co-pays and deductibles right away.*

Here's the punchline of this article: *With so much less money going to providers, the cuts could have major impacts on patient access to health care, such as fewer physicians accepting Medicare patients.*

So, you come to me, and you say, 'Daniel, I need $100,000.' I say, 'Okay, well let's look at that.' Here's your portfolio. Your current total asset value is $432,000. That's what you have access to. Now, because these are all annuities and IRAs, we were able to grow these very nicely, tax deferred. So, we're building up all these gains inside of your accounts, right? However, the taxes must be paid first to access your money. So, we need $100,000, right?

Let's look at how much you've contributed. You've put in this much here. This would be your cost basis. That's the amount of money you put in. So, we add these numbers up.

You've put in $100,000 of your own money, and so that tells me that the first $332,000 that comes out is fully taxable. We have to pay the taxes on that to access it."

My Beloved Client: "Okay."

Daniel: "If we need $100,000 of fully-taxable money in one year, what would that do to your income tax return? You have pensions and Social Security. Imagine dropping $100,000 of fully-taxable income into your return at some point in the future if we have higher taxes…"

My Beloved Client: "It's going to raise everything!"

Daniel: "You're going to pay a lot of unnecessary income tax. With your income, you might really need to take $120,000 or $130,000 just for me to get to your $100,000."

My Beloved Client: "Yep. Sure. I'm with you."

Daniel: "So now, you have to pull out $130,000 — $30,000 just to pay the income taxes. Now, we're left with $300,000 going forward, and you paid an unnecessary $30,000 in income tax. So, let me ask you a question. If you had to pay an exorbitant amount of unnecessary income tax at a time when you need your money the most, does that feel like tax reform to you?"

My Beloved Client: "No."

Daniel: "Right? Isn't that like being held hostage by the taxes? So, what are we going to do to make sure this doesn't happen to you?"

My Beloved Client: "I don't know. What should I do?"

Daniel: "Well, maybe we should consider tax diversification. We spent so much time doing investment diversification. Everybody knows instinctively not to put all your eggs into one basket. We diversify, right?

My Beloved Client: "Right."

Daniel: "It makes sense. We know, instinctively, we want to spread it around amongst different companies and advisors. So, why aren't we doing that with your taxes? Why are we betting on all tax-deferred dollars at a time when we know the government's going to need money the most? Isn't that risky?"

My Beloved Client: "Yeah, I suppose it really is."

Daniel: "So, maybe we should pursue a path of offering you some tax-free money when you need that money first. Let me show you IRS Publication 525 and how we would do that.

Here is IRS Publication 525 Cat. No. 15047D, the most overlooked provision of the tax code by my estimate. It's called, *Taxable and Nontaxable Income.*

Right here on page 22, it describes Accelerated Death Benefits. *Certain amounts paid as accelerated death benefits under a life insurance contract or viatical settlement before the insured's death are excluded from income if the insured is terminally or chronically ill.*

So, let's apply these provisions to your scenario with a real-word strategy.

This is today. If you need $100,000. You have $432,000, $100,000 of it's yours, $332,000 is taxable. If you need that $100,000, you pay $30,000 of unnecessary income tax, and your money is reduced significantly. But, let's look at this with tax diversification.

By taking out one to 2% of these fully taxable gains and reclassifying them, I can add about $200,000 to $250,000 of tax-free leverage on to this portfolio for you. Let me show you what it looks like.

Your $432,000 fully taxable, now looks like $682,000, and the first $250,000 comes out tax-free. So, let's run through this scenario again. You need $100,000 from this portfolio where it is using tax diversification. Now, you have $582,000 still available to you, and somebody else still picks up the check for your healthcare."

CURRENT TAXABLE EVENT SUMMARY	
Federal Rate: 24% | State Rate: 6%	
CURRENT VALUE	$432,000 IRA (Fully Taxable)
NEED	$100,000
TAXES OWED	$30,000
REMAINING VALUE	$302,000

CURRENT TAXABLE EVENT SUMMARY	
Federal Rate: 24% | State Rate: 6%	
CURRENT VALUE	$432,000 IRA (Fully Taxable)
TAX-FREE LEVERAGE	$250,000 (Tax-Free)
NEW VALUE	$682,000
NEED	$100,000
TAXES OWED	$0
REMAINING VALUE	$582,000

I'm going to pause the conversation here before the disclaimer for the example above, and before the CPAs and CFPs gather in an angry mob with pitchforks. Again, we do not know what the future holds for tax law, deductions, and rates. This tax summary obviously is not accurate for today's tax code, laws, and environment. This is just a conversation for us to have a simple discussion about the future unknowns of tax risk and rising health care costs. Obviously, there currently are marginal and effective rates. There are medical deductions and all of this depends on the client's income, filing status, and other factors. We are merely asking people how they feel about having all their life savings exposed to these unknowns when they need to count on that money to take care of them. That is it. It's an example not an actual conversation. However, I have included a CPA's analysis of a scenario for today's tax environment and a potential future scenario taking into account the progressive nature, true effective rate, and medical expense deductibility. This will be presented later in the book.

*For illustrative purposes only. Actual results may vary. Assumes certain income and deductions. Uses an average of state rates for applicability. This is only an example to have a conversation around a scenario where tax rates go up, deductions go down, or medical deductions are eliminated completely. There is a CPA's analysis of a current projection taking into account the true progressive nature of the taxable impact for an accurate Federal and state assumption considering the current deductibility for medical expenses. It also includes two different income scenarios and a projection of what the expense could be if taxes were to double.

Now back to the conversations...

Remember the punchline to the article I shared with you? Look at what the director of AARP says, "We're deeply concerned that the tax proposal being made will very directly affect the ability of Medicare to maintain services, and we do not think it's fair that older-age Americans have to pay for Medicare their entire working lives and get stuck with the bill for this tax overhaul." You already paid your Medicare premiums; is it fair that now they're going to come after you for the bill again? Wouldn't it be wise to make sure somebody else still pays for your healthcare for you and ensures that it's done in the most tax-efficient way possible?"

My Beloved Client: "Tell me, how do I do that? "

Daniel: "Well, let me tell you the catch first, okay? Because I've told you all the good parts. This isn't something where we can say, 'Daniel, I love this. Let's just do this right now.' You must qualify. Because the policy has accelerated death benefits attached to it, for me to add these benefits on top of your annuities and IRAs for you, we must see if you qualify. Let me outline the process.

We submit an application. Then, a nurse will come to your house to conduct a physical. She does blood, urine, and an EKG test. She will ask you some questions about your current doctor and your health history. Do you have any pressing health concerns?"

My Beloved Client: "No."

Daniel: "Okay. She does a physical. Then, the company writes to your doctor and requests your medical records. The entire process takes about two-and-a-half months. So, eight to ten weeks later, we get back together. If they made me an offer in writing, we sit down at that meeting and decide, does this make good financial sense for your family? Do you like the offer? Is this something that we want to do? You don't have to make any decisions today. I don't even know if we can do this, but wouldn't it be wise to at least see if you qualify because there's no cost or obligation to find out? If we get an offer in two-and-a-half months, then we sit back down and say okay, let's do this, and if I don't think it's a good offer, I'll be the first one to tell you we shouldn't do it."

My Beloved Client: "Okay, but if they make the offer, what am I doing?"

Daniel: "At that point, we would take one to 2% of these gains, reclassify them, and do some diversification into a unique, special type of life insurance policy that provides that leveraged benefit of approximately 50% of your current portfolio to you while you're alive to stave off those expenses from damaging your current savings and the future income for you and your spouse."

My Beloved Client: "Can you tell me how much that is, or…"

Daniel: "Sure. On $432,000, we're looking at approximately $4,000 to $8,000."

My Beloved Client: "A year?"

Daniel: "Every year, but let me ask you a question. These IRAs are all making between 6% to 7% a year, right?"

My Beloved Client: "Right. "

Daniel: "If I couldn't make you one to 2%, would you want to work with me?"

My Beloved Client: "Ha ha, No."

Daniel: "So, if I could use only one to 2% of just your gains every year, not your principal, but rather than reinvesting them into the same strategy compounding the tax problem, instead, make sure we add another $250,000 tax-free, making your $432,000 look like $682,000 at that meeting, then we could decide if that makes sense. But that's putting the cart before the horse. Maybe we should see if it's even viable for you. Without knowing if you can get an offer, there is no way you can make an informed decision. By seeing if this strategy works for you, I'll be doing the best possible job I can for you. If it does, then we'll get back together and make those decisions at that meeting. Will that be okay?"

My Beloved Client: "Absolutely."

Daniel: "Okay. I need you for five more minutes to do an application."

My Beloved Client: "Let's give it a shot."

*The conversation above is an example for illustrative purposes only. All actual client conversations are privileged and will remain confidential. This should not be considered to be specific advice in any way for your individual situation. This is not an exact representation of how I speak to my clients directly. This is just an example of how to walk through a simple concise process to determine vast economic issues and then be able to analyze your situation to determine how prepared you are appropriately.

Next, it provides a simple illustration to assist you to decide if you would like to possibly evaluate potential options if you feel it would be helpful regarding the afore-mentioned risks. The representation of the taxable events are not accurate, but the full accurate representation is provided by a professional and licensed CPA later in this book. This is done to simply allow for realistic conversation only, not full analysis at this stage. That comes throughout the underwriting process only be the properly licensed professionals. Remember, we are doing our best to have a conversation around future law and tax changes that don't exist right now. Also, if you do have pressing health concerns, there may still be other options besides this specific strategy. Speak with your qualified financial professional to discuss those options.

This is arguably going to be one of the most important conversations in the next ten years for most retirees who are not properly tax diversified. That's it. Congratulations! You're done with the book. Thank you for reading my life's work. This is as simple as I can make it. If you're dying to see if you qualify for an offer to your retirement like this, then put this book down and call the agent that gave it to you. They truly care enough about you to broach this conversation with you, and more importantly, they are the only financial professional licensed and qualified to help you with this specific problem.

Do not call me unless I am the one who gave you the book. I did not write this book to attract clients or sell life insurance. I am only one man with a finite amount of time. This book was meant to be a depth charge, sending iceberg-shattering tidal waves across the Atlantic. You can send me messages in bottles back from paradise —hopefully containing nothing more than thank you cards complaining you're running out of rum and that you have to go because the limbo line is forming. I do not want to receive any distressed messages asking for help after it is too late. This book is supposed to prevent that!

Now, if you're not so convinced, or if you think there's more to the story, there is—much more. In fact, if you're intrigued, I invite you to continue reading. But I caution you, if you're a worrier like me, then what I'm about to share with you will shake you to your core because the basis of my theory will absolutely rock the notion that this country is fiscally sound and that our economy is booming. It is on course to inevitably crash into an iceberg. I'm talking of course about our country's true national emergency, the rapidly spreading infection to our financial health, our national debt. While COVID-19 has shaken our economy, the economic impact we will eventual feel from the debt has not even occurred yet.

KEY TAKEAWAYS FROM CHAPTER TWO: THE CONVERSATION

- Be proactive. The last thing you want to say, or for you have to ask your current team of professionals is, "Why didn't you tell me about this before it happened?"

- Medicare is one of the few entitlements that the government can touch. So, if they take out 40% of the budget for Medicare, do you think healthcare will be less expensive in your retirement or more expensive?

- AARP says, "We're deeply concerned that the tax proposal being made will very directly affect the ability of Medicare to maintain services, and we do not think it's fair that older-age Americans have to pay for Medicare their entire working lives and get stuck with the bill for this tax overhaul."

- The three largest budget items in our national debt are Medicare and Medicaid, Social Security, and Defense and War. Medicare is the largest budget item. Budget cuts could have major impacts on patient access to healthcare, such as fewer physicians accepting Medicare patients.

- Everybody understands not to put all your eggs into one basket. Maybe we should consider tax diversification. Taking out one to 2% of fully-taxable gains and reclassifying them can add tax-free leverage to a portfolio.

- Remember, you have to qualify for the unique, special type of life insurance policy that provides that leveraged benefit. You qualify with your health.

- Publication 525 allows you to distribute significant amounts of an insurance company's money back to yourself in exchange for pennies on the dollar in the form of 1-2% of your current interest.

- First, see if it's even viable for you. Without knowing if you can get an offer, there is no way you can make an informed decision. By seeing if this strategy works for you, you'll be doing the best possible job to secure your retirement from this risk. If it does, then get back together and make those decisions at that meeting.

- Call the person that gave you the book for more information that can be helpful to your unique situation.

Oh, look attorneys, another disclaimer. Aren't you proud of me?

Remember, everyone's situation is unique to them. The strategies they use and advice they seek should be by licensed professionals only and should be specific to their individual situation.

Health, life expectancy, family history, genetics, financial condition, balances sheets, income statements, time horizon, risk capacity, objective, past experience, present knowledge and all of the material facts are considerations when choosing the right strategy and professional to help you with it. While the example above contained a sample scenario, it is nothing more than that. It is for the purpose of having a conversation about the potentially threatening combination of higher taxes and a catastrophic healthcare event to someone with all of their liquid savings in tax-deferred accounts. Diversity and this specific tool are possibilities but never the only option.

This is also describing a possible future scenario that does not exist yet. This is an interpretation of possible outcomes as they may result from the increasing national debt and the Governments methods of dealing with it.

Please consider that there is no such thing as blanket help, meaning that you cannot say that one solution is right for every scenario. Again, this book is to be interpreted in no way as any form of advice for your retirement. Seek your own professional guidance when deploying a specific strategy learned from this book. Thank you.

Chapter Three: The Reality

"One hundred percent of what is collected is absorbed solely by the interest on the federal debt and by Federal Government contributions to transfer payments. In other words, all individual income tax revenues are gone before one nickel is spent on the services which the taxpayers expect from their government."
— The Grace Commission, 1982

"I was reading in the paper today that Congress wants to replace the dollar bill with a coin. They've already done it. It's called a nickel."
— Jay Leno

"I sincerely believe that banking establishments are more dangerous than standing armies, and that the principle of spending money to be paid by posterity, under the name of funding, is but swindling futurity on a large scale."
— Thomas Jefferson

"You can entitle this the relief for the rich act."
—Warren Buffet, PBS interview, June 27th, 2017

"We will pay for this tax reform, these stimulus packages, and corporate bailouts one day when the debt gets too high. The only way to have a chance to come out ahead is to take advantage of the low rates today! While we have it, tax reform should not be short-term savings; it should be harvesting gains and reclassifying for future tax-free use. Do not miss this harvest!"
—Daniel Rondberg

"I own plenty of life insurance," I said with a sheepish grin. "My wife and I are young and about the same age. If I were to die today, she'd have a long way to go, and do you think I want her to remarry and be happy? No! I want her to be miserable and rich."

The whole room laughed. Well, how about that? I felt extremely relieved. I couldn't wait to tell my wife.

The reality is that if nothing were to change for you in retirement, you would be fine. You've learned to live within your means at this point. You're a good steward of your money. You have a retirement income that provides more than you spend, and typically, the average person does not retire and then spend a large chunk of their net worth randomly on a Ferrari, right? You've formed financial habits and behaviors your entire life, and it's ingrained a standard of living into you that fits your personality.

If nothing serious happens, you'll be fine, and you don't need guys like me. In fact, if you make a 2% return or a 7% return, it really won't impact your lifestyle year to year because you have good income. However, we all focus way too much on the micro. What are the returns this calendar year? We magnify that as our standard for a good indicator of our financial success so much that we rarely focus on the macro. What scenario could occur and force the plan to change? What could cause you to break your spending limits and force you to start withdrawing large amounts of your principal? Wouldn't a catastrophic incident involving your health be the only major life event capable of such powerful magnitude?

In fact, 50% of all bankruptcies in this country are due to health-care bills from these events. Here is another fact: if we live long enough, there is roughly a 70% chance we will become disabled and need some type of care. (Longtermcare.gov) There is also a 100% chance we are going to die one day. I'm sorry to be a downer, but none of us are getting out of this alive. If there is a 70% chance we'll need care, and 100% chance that we'll die leaving behind a loved one that might need care, shouldn't we plan for that?

What DO care costs amount to these days? Well, here are the facts:

- HealthView Services: In the next ten years, American's will need 90% of their social security check to cover their health-care costs. (http://www.hvsfinancial.com)

- SkilledNursing.org: The national average for weekly (44 hours) home healthcare is $3,813. ($15,252/month!) (https://www.skillednursingfacilities.org/resources/nursin g-home-costs/)

- FightChronicDisease.org: Chronic illnesses account for 75% of the $2.2 trillion we spend on healthcare each year in the U.S.

Let's summarize the problem again: Fidelity creates a report every year listing the average 401(k) balance in the United States. Do you know what it was for the second quarter of 2019? It was $106,000. Plus, we just saw that the nonpartisan government re-sources and nonprofits are literally flashing warning signs and suggesting amounts to realistically plan for in retirement.

1. There's not enough money.

   The amount that is saved is stuck inside of a qualified account, or, in other words, all pre-tax. This means that since you've never paid taxes on any of this money, it isn't fully yours. The Internal Revenue Service is your partner in this account. In exchange for a lien on that account, they lent you the money you would have normally had to pay in taxes during those contribution years while you were working. Therefore, they will get their money back at the time of distribution.

2. The money that we do have is not fully ours.

3. Finally, you are entering or have already entered retirement, and there is no time to make more money.

What do you do? What strategy will help you if you're in this scenario? Well, this is why the value of leverage is so crucial, and what is the only financial tool that can take small amounts of money and create leverage by turning them into instant guaranteed amounts of larger money to use? A special type of life insurance with an accelerated death benefit rider. There is even a special provision for this in the tax code. Publication 525 has a small "hidden" exemption. (Ok, it's not really hidden, its right there on page 22 of the 2019 IRS Publication 525 Cat. No. 15047D Taxable and Non-taxable Income (Rev. February 2020).

But they allow you to maximize this exemption by using this type of life insurance. You can literally turn one $500 premium into $500,000 tax-free. Now when I say hidden, let's be practical. How many Americans have thoroughly read all 1.3 million-something pages of the U.S. tax code? A coincidence? I don't believe so. So, what is life insurance? It's leverage. It's instant estate. It's access to money that you didn't have before. Why is that so important? Well, consider the problem. What are most Americans supposed to do when:

- They don't have enough money,

- What money they do have is not fully theirs,

- There is no time to make more?

If they could diversify just 2% of their gains (not their principal) to add 50% or more to their estate that can pay for this specific need, instead of compounding the problem, why wouldn't they, at least, investigate if this is a viable strategy since there is zero cost or obligation?

I have a test for every single pundit out there. Other than insurance like long-term care, cancer insurance, etc., show me one other financial vehicle that can offer this type of tax-free access of someone else's money to immediately pay for these expenses all on a guaranteed basis. Go ahead, I'll wait. You cannot. That's because this is the job for a special type of life insurance policy. As economist Tom Hegna says, "It's not the job of mutual funds, ETFs, real estate, gold, or bonds, just like life insurance shouldn't pretend to do the job of any of those vehicles, it has a specific job."

In fact, I think that it goes against everything we are taught from day one as financial professionals to recommend anything other than what most appropriately fits the need of the client's objectives based on their circumstances. It is transparently self-serving to persuade people that anything else can do the job of life insurance.

There is a new buzzword in the financial community—fiduciary. Everybody is so concerned about whether you hold the fiduciary standard.

Tom Hegna is the leading retirement expert in the world. He has written four of the top retirement books ever sold, and all of them include a recommendation to use insurance. When it comes to his outlook on the fiduciary standard, he argues that if the same story problem I outlined above was given to 100 different fiduciaries, the result would be 100 different "recommendations." How can that be? Fiduciaries are supposed to do the "best" thing for the clients' interests, but "best" means one not 100.

Another bizarre contradiction of the fiduciary standard Hegna points out is that there is currently no mechanism to enforce these fiduciaries other than being sued by clients. Well, how prohibitive are legal costs in these matters? Not to mention the time and stress of dragging out litigation. Finally, fiduciaries are also not doing a good job of recommending life insurance to neutralizing the key risk that it's meant to manage. How can any financial recommendation be complete without assessing all the key risks with the proper tools? The only tool that is suitable to fit this particular need is life insurance or another form of insurance if you cannot self-insure and don't want to go on state aid.

I am not against fiduciaries. I am against clients not getting what they need when they expect to be taken care of and they trust a professional to help them plan for any situation. This happens with clients of fiduciaries and clients of life insurance agents every single day. Not all fiduciaries are life insurance agents, and not all life insurance agents are fiduciaries. Here in lies the disconnect.

There are fiduciaries who make the best recommendations they can for their clients. Remember they are bound by law to act in their clients' best interest. A governing board oversees their actions. I've had many new clients come into my office over the years who have had no discussion of what they want to happen when they get sick, nor what they want to happen when they die.

Life insurance is a tax-free safe haven that can immediately flush someone else's money into your estate for these qualifying medical events. If you fall into the 30% that don't need care, you can pass all that leveraged money to a surviving spouse tax-free in the form of a death benefit so they may use that money for their own care should the need arise.

Why would the IRS be so concerned about framing and classifying the use of these tax-free benefits if they were not extremely powerful? Remember, the IRS cares very much how much money goes into any one life insurance policy; this is demonstrated with the TAMRA, DEFRA, and TEFRA guidelines that outline funding and modified endowment contracts (when the funding of a life insurance contract surpasses the limit set according to federal tax laws). Whoa, whoa! Too much jargon! Here's the punchline: if there weren't amazing benefits involved, why would they care?

Ed Slott, famous CPA and America's number one IRA Advisor, has been saying it on PBS for years, "The single, biggest benefit in the tax code today is the tax-free exemption for life insurance." Need the proof? Look at IRS publication 525 titled *Taxable and Non-Taxable Income* found on IRS.gov. The accelerated death benefit is clearly shown to be paid out completely tax-free either in the event of death as a lump sum to the beneficiary or in payments to the owner while alive if chronically ill. "

I've shared this publication in banquet halls and offices filled with financial professionals all over the country and I can tell you from my experience, less than 10% have read the text. So, if they aren't reading and practicing it, who the heck is? Well… you! The top CPA and IRA advisor in the country says it's the best exemption in the tax code.

Now I want to tread carefully in this next paragraph for all my readers who are dedicated to financial education that specifically tells you to buy only term insurance and no guaranteed policies. Please understand, I have a tremendous amount of respect for true financial educators. I think some courses have helped a lot of people and changed lives with their reach and dedication. I am not here to step on anyone's beliefs. I will just say one thing about the scope of the life insurance conversation. When finding the right term to help a family and not using whole life or other life insurance for that specific need, I think they are doing their best to look out for their followers. I will also say that there are different types of life insurance for different reasons. Some educators are masters of motivating people to take action and change their behavior—two of the hardest things in the world to get people to do, even when it's for the purpose of bettering their lives. Do you think they can do that by giving several complicated choices to people who struggle to manage their own finances? No, they must create sacred boundaries, a simple do and don't guide to follow without question.

This guide is the only way they are successful in helping anyone, and they feel the good outweighs the sacrifice. I get that. However, choosing to narrow the scope on two important factors regarding this topic has created two consequences.

First, people are often told not to even look at care benefits from insurance until age 59, and then to shop it aggressively. Sadly, because you must qualify for care benefit policies (and life insurance policies with accelerated death benefit riders) based on your health, by age 59, some people have already had a life event such as cancer or cardiac issues that would prevent receiving an offer to accept this coverage. If an offer for coverage can be extended after an event like this has already occurred, often it is modified or a rated premium making it too expensive. I cannot tell you how many people practically beg for these solutions after they are no longer a reality. Anyone who has practiced will tell you that the truth of our business is if you call us coverage denied, if we call you coverage approved. The sad truth is that not everyone can use these options because their health history prevents them from qualifying. It is not fair, but it is true. These conversations are among some of the most difficult I have ever had. Waiting until age 59 just isn't the right move for everyone.

Second, some potentially harmful dialogue has been created, and I hear over and over, "I don't need life insurance. I have assets.

If it isn't term, it is a rip-off!" The fact is, term is only temporary, and less that 2% of policies pay a claim. So, it is very unlikely you will be able to use it in this situation. While you may have assets, ask yourself: Do you want to be forced to sell those assets in potentially your most vulnerable physical or mental condition you've ever experienced? Or would you rather someone else pay for these expenses to take care of you during this time?

Another thing I want to mention is that Jim Harbaugh, head football coach at Michigan, and his advisors, insisted the university pay Jim with a cash-value life insurance policy, making him one of the highest-paid head coaches in college sports[1]. Again, why would they do this if it was a rip off? I don't want to disappoint anyone reading out there, but spoiler alert, Jim Harbaugh does not call me for guidance. However, the strategies his advisors used were based around the tax exemptions and structure that life insurance provides, and it is not a term policy.

Also, please understand I am not bad-mouthing or, more importantly, misrepresenting the message of these financial educators in any way. I don't have one negative thing to say about them. I am simply pointing out the two areas surrounding this topic that I hear about most during this conversation. Although I am hearing it from their followers, I understand that it may not reflect anything that was actually said or taught in their courses. Financial products are neither bad nor good. They are tools, and each of them was created for a specific job. Find the right tool for the right job provided by the right professional, and your results should be successful. Execution plays a big role in the measure of your success as well.

---

[1] https://www.espn.com/college-football/story/_/id/17332547/michigan-wolverines-jim-harbaugh-agree-increased-compensation-form-life-insurance-loan

Remember, nothing you read in this book is my opinion. Everything you read in this book is carefully designed to be based on facts and data. I use only nonpartisan and nonprofit reports to bring you the most accurate and unbiased data available. This book will serve as a resource with each paragraph carefully written to contain nothing but valuable quotes, data, and facts that will serve as a reference for your conversation with your advisors going forward.

Now, if you're saying, "Daniel, hold on, my advisor recommended long-term care insurance, and I've been carrying a policy for a long time. What about long-term care? "Well, then you have even more reason to continue reading as I will demonstrate, using the website LongTermCare.acl.gov, that this book can still be of great assistance to you.

To be clear, long-term care insurance is another tool that can create leverage and pay out tax-free for this event. It too can have a death benefit. However, the reason we are discussing life insurance is because with Americans living longer than ever, the need for long-term care will continue to grow at an unsuitable rate, causing the number of care claims to continue to rise and forcing the companies to pass those costs to policy holders in the form of astronomical premium increases. Consider this Kiplinger article that states, "Almost all long-term-care insurance companies have raised customers' premiums years after they bought their policies, with average increases of 50% to 60% over the past decade, says Kevin McCarty, the former commissioner of the Florida Office of Insurance Regulation."

Unfortunately, many people will not be able to afford to carry those policies with much-higher premiums. Life insurance can be set up with a guarantee that your premiums will never increase. This will protect you for the premium you agreed upon for the rest of your life. Am I saying one is better than the other? No. Both are important and have different strengths and weaknesses. Each should be evaluated by you and your agent for creating a complete solution. That is the reality. Also, there are incredible long-term care/life insurance hybrid products with guaranteed no-increase premium structures and complete return of premium guaranteed riders available. I will discuss those later in the Bonus sections.

Key Takeaways from CHAPTER THREE: THE REALITY

- If nothing were to change for you in retirement, you would be fine. You've learned to live within your means at this point. But ask yourself, "What scenario could force the plan to change? What could cause me to break my spending limits and require me to start withdrawing large amounts of my principal?"

- Fifty percent of all bankruptcies in this country are a result of healthcare bills from these events.

- There is roughly a 70% chance we will become disabled and need some type of care.

- There is a 100% chance we are going to die one day.

- Fidelity reported that the average 401(k) balance in the United States for the second quarter of 2019 was $106,000.

- 401(k) savings are stuck inside of a qualified account, or in other words, you pay the tax at the future tax rate at the time of your withdrawal.

- Since we've never paid taxes on any of the money in a 401(k), it isn't fully ours.

- We are running out of time and options.

- It goes against everything we are taught from day one as financial professionals to recommend anything other than what most appropriately fits the need of the client's objectives based on their circumstances. It is transparently self-serving to persuade people that anything else can do the job of life insurance.

- Unfortunately, many people will not be able to afford to carry the much higher premiums long-term care could soon face. Life insurance can be set up with a guarantee that your premiums will never increase protecting you for the agreed upon premium for life.

- The solution is the job for a special type of life insurance policy. Just like life insurance shouldn't pretend to do the job of other financial vehicles, it has a specific job.

- Do you want to be forced to sell your assets in potentially your most vulnerable physical or mental condition you've ever experienced? Or would you rather someone else pay for these expenses to take care of you during this time?

- Financial products are neither bad nor good. They are tools, and each of them was created for a specific job. Find the right tool for the right job provided by the right professional, and your results should be successful. Execution plays a big role in the measure of your success as well.

- Long-term care insurance should be properly evaluated by you and a licensed health agent. I do not discuss long-term care insurance in this book, but you should carefully consider your options when looking to remove care as a risk to your retirement. Also, review them with a qualified professional who specializes in long-term care solutions

Chapter Four: The Proof

"The biggest threat is the unknown tax impact of future rates and deductibility. I lived through the highest marginal tax rates, and it is not unforeseeable that we could see those times again."
— Mark Renberg, CPA

"A single four-letter word would explain why higher tax rates are inevitable: Math. Tax rates would likely have to double to liquidate our nation's debt and pay for underfunded entitlement programs such as Social Security and Medicare."
— David Walker, Former United States Comptroller General

"We just saw the government increase our national debt by more than 20% in a few weeks. What happens when they start bailing out industries and pension funds? Who is going to ultimately end up paying for that?"
—Daniel Rondberg

"You are the only people in the United States who can help people retiring with this problem!" I boomed.

As the veins in my neck began to bulge, my eyebrows raised and my face flushed red. My hands flew around the stage, and I moved purposefully and frantically, begging for these advisors to listen. 150 heads whipped toward the front of the room. No one was texting or taking notes. I had their attention.

"When did bankruptcy and state aid become acceptable forms of healthcare planning for our seniors? Is that really how we are going to show respect to the greatest generation of our county?

I'm sorry, but we should be ashamed of ourselves. We can't even do our jobs with the greatest tools ever available to prevent grandmas and grandpas from spending their final days neglected and confined. Look, I'll be honest: some people will be harmed by what it is going to cost to fix the problem in this county. It's just not going to be my clients, and it shouldn't be yours either."

— Excerpt from my first speech at the Fidelis Consultants training summit in 2018 in Denver, Colorado

Remember, I said that if you didn't believe me, I would prove to you that you are currently sitting on a cruise ship, enjoying a five-course gourmet meal, unknowingly riding full steam ahead on the slowest moving shipwreck known in U.S. history called "your retirement's reaction to our country's national debt?" Ok, I don't think I used those exact words, but if you need proof and lots of it, or if you're saying to yourself, "Show me this data. I want the facts," well then you have arrived at your chapter because I'm going to provide more facts in this chapter than an encyclopedia. (Not literally, this book would have to be at least three times bigger than this. Can a guy not create a metaphor and then back it up with a Zoolander reference? See, a book about taxes and the economy can be fun.) Now, here's a quick trivia question: in the popular 90's sitcom *Friends*, which volume did Joey purchase from the traveling Encyclopedia salesman when he could only afford one book? If you said "V," you are correct, and you're still paying attention. Thank you for that. Let's proceed.

If you're more of a story learner and you're looking for some entertainment with the facts, then might I recommend you skip ahead to Chapter Five: My Theory. It's full of equal facts and truths, but frankly, it won't be as dry as this chapter.

What I'm about to hit you with is over 2,000 hours of research and data condensed down into a presentation I give when I speak at a college or community center. I've also included the survey I use that you can fill out as we go through it to determine your current preparedness in dealing with this risk. So, for you academics out there, extend your index finger, and put it to the bridge of your nose to properly push up your taped-together glasses. I'm also going to give you a professional third-party, CPA audit of my tax-diversification client example from Chapter Two at the end of this chapter.

The following is a transcript of one of my live seminars:

Tonight, the title of my course is called "Time Bomb." That's kind of an ominous title. I know what you're thinking, who brought this guy here? That is kind of a bummer. It's a title chosen because the effects, the economic impact of this tax reform that was just passed, will be a long, slow, drawn-out process that we won't really know the outcome of for many years to come—the real outcome that is.

We want to help people be proactive in finding solutions. In December 2017, Congress passed the tax reform, and I believe that day changed almost everybody's retirement. We need to bring a lot of awareness to this subject.

This evening, we're going to talk about tax reform, how to take advantage of it, and what it's going to mean for the cost of care in your retirement. More specifically, what it will cost you if you need to use your fully-taxable retirement savings to make up for large sums of care costs. We're going to talk a lot about the economics of what's happening and try to give as much information as possible so you can really be informed about what's happening. But I promise you, there will be a silver lining and a solution in there, as well as something encouraging so you can take advantage of this opportunity.

I put together a five-question survey so we can go through the information together, and you can determine for yourself how well prepared you feel for what's currently happening. There's a lot happening right now, and the news cycle is so fast. I could name a few events that have recently occurred but you have probably forgotten because there's so much else happening.

Survey Question 1

On a scale from one to 10:

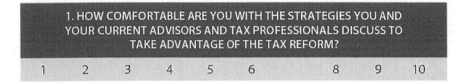

1. HOW COMFORTABLE ARE YOU WITH THE STRATEGIES YOU AND YOUR CURRENT ADVISORS AND TAX PROFESSIONALS DISCUSS TO TAKE ADVANTAGE OF THE TAX REFORM?								
1	2	3	4	5	6	8	9	10

Take a minute to mark your answer on a sheet of paper or in this book. One is "not comfortable" at all, and 10 is "extremely comfortable." Notice that you can't mark number seven. People always ask me, "Why not?" The reason is because it's a non-committal answer. Seven is very safe. If you choose seven, you're saying, "I'm okay." But if you choose six, that's barely passing, and that's not very good. If you choose eight, that means you're doing pretty well. I avoid seven so we can make a good indication as to how you're currently feeling.

Next, I'll share a few more independent resources that we can pull from to get some information, such as the Congressional budget office, non-partisan financial analysis and economic outlook.

Sequestration

A new buzzword has been introduced for some of us—sequestration.

Sequestration is basically when you are given a benefit over here, and there's an equal tax cut happening behind the scenes over there. So, while we're watching the news and celebrating all the booming businesses and the bonuses being given out, people are going to get larger tax refunds, but there will be cuts.

Consider this article from AARP: https://www.aarp.org/politics-society/advocacy/info-2017/senate -tax-medicare-cuts-fd.html

Medicare is subject to "pay-as-you-go" (PAYGO) laws which is why this article raises so much concern.

The AARP article states, "The tax measure would prompt the law, commonly referred to as PAYGO. The law was designed to keep the deficit in check by requiring the administration to institute spending cuts in many mandatory federal programs if Congress passes any measure that increases the deficit but doesn't include offsetting revenues."

Taxpolicycenter.org states, "PAYGO, which stands for "pay as you go," is a budget rule requiring that (using current law as the baseline) tax cuts, as well as increases in entitlement and other mandatory spending, must be offset by tax increases or cuts in mandatory spending.[2]"

They also define sequestration as, "the action of taking legal possession of assets until a debt has been paid or other claims have been met." The money is coming from somewhere, and the sequestration really clues us into where it's coming from—it's coming from the budget for Medicare!

---

[2] https://www.taxpolicycenter.org/briefing-book/what-paygo

Survey Question 2

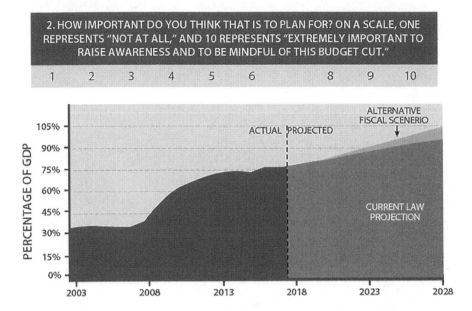

Here's an example from the report that Congress was asked to create after the tax reform. It happened quickly, and the special committee that was formed asked, the budget office this:

"We want you to determine what the country is going look like 10 years from now running on this tax reform. What is it going to do for growth? Because there are some good benefits in there for growth. What is it going to do for our debt?"

I am including what they projected in this report here. It's a huge report, but what they found in this example is that over the next 10 years, a trillion dollars will be added to the debt each year. Every... single... year. By an economist's definition, it is going to be runaway debt, which means it's going too fast, and we can't really keep up with it. It could be the first time in history that we experience runaway debt.

This report highlighted, "For the first time in 30 years, we're going to have a 105% debt to GDP growth." So what does that mean? Take a look at this graph below.

WILL TAXES INCREASE?

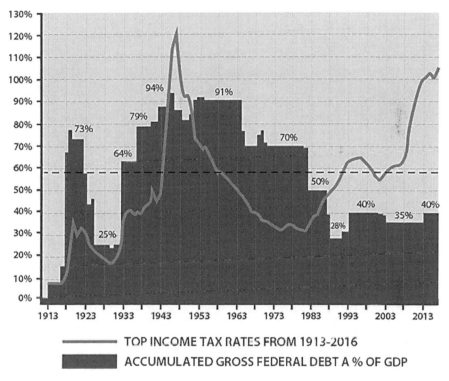

TOP INCOME TAX RATES FROM 1913-2016

ACCUMULATED GROSS FEDERAL DEBT A % OF GDP

This is a very interesting graph that shows the tax rates in the United States for the last 100 years. You can see at one point, the highest bracket we ever had was 94%, which is really, really high. And what it's showing is a trend: the light grey line is gross federal debt as a percentage of GDP. So what you can see is that as the debt and GDP increase as a percentage, we typically see higher tax rates. We've had a nice run where debt has been low for about 50 years, and now we're seeing debt start to creep back up to 105% of GDP growth. If you look at the last 100 years in the United States, logic would tell you what kind of tax rates will probably follow. We don't know, but based on this information, it shows that there's a possibility.

Take a break or review those graphics one more time. When you're ready, please move on to the next question.

Survey Question 3

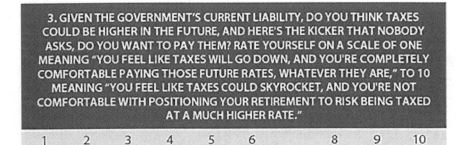

3. GIVEN THE GOVERNMENT'S CURRENT LIABILITY, DO YOU THINK TAXES COULD BE HIGHER IN THE FUTURE, AND HERE'S THE KICKER THAT NOBODY ASKS, DO YOU WANT TO PAY THEM? RATE YOURSELF ON A SCALE OF ONE MEANING "YOU FEEL LIKE TAXES WILL GO DOWN, AND YOU'RE COMPLETELY COMFORTABLE PAYING THOSE FUTURE RATES, WHATEVER THEY ARE," TO 10 MEANING "YOU FEEL LIKE TAXES COULD SKYROCKET, AND YOU'RE NOT COMFORTABLE WITH POSITIONING YOUR RETIREMENT TO RISK BEING TAXED AT A MUCH HIGHER RATE."

| 1 | 2 | 3 | 4 | 5 | 6 | | 8 | 9 | 10 |

Below are a couple of resources for you, and I want to stop here and tell you again, I'm not a conspiracy theorist, I'm not a doom-sayer, I'm not a whistle blower, and I'm not a crazy author. I just read all the information that is freely available. I don't think a lot of financial professionals do, and they are missing out on crucial information. What all this is telling me is that the economists and government are issuing warning signs and saying, "Hey, pay attention! Something is going to happen."

The Social Security and Medicare trustees put out a new report every May. In the report from 2018[3], the trustees project the HI Trust Fund (the main trust for Medicare) will be depleted by 2026, three years earlier than they projected in last year's report.

At that time, dedicated revenues will be sufficient to pay 91% of HI costs. The Trustees project that the share of HI costs that can

[3]Social Security And Medicare Trustees Report: A Summary of the 2018 Annuals Report - www.ssa.gov/OACT/TR/2018

be financed with HI-dedicated revenues will decline slowly to 78% in 2039 and will then rise gradually to 85% in 2092. The HI fund again fails the test of short-range financial adequacy, as its trust fund ratio is already below 100% of annual costs and is expected to decline continuously until reserve depletion in 2026.

The trustees are the people in charge of the budget, and they were wrong by three years just a year ago.

How is this going to impact us, though? It will impact us through cost of care. HealthView Services, another phenomenal independent retirement cost service analysis of health care costs and retirement, is telling people to plan for health care costs in retirement as follows.

	Life Expectancy	Medical Expenses in Final Two Years without End-of-Life Costs	Additional Cost Hospitalization	Additional Cost Doctors & Tests	Additional Cost Prescription Drugs	Medical Expenses in Final Two Years with End-of-Life Costs	Difference (%)
Male	87	$132,459	$908	$2,291	$3,923	$139,582	+5.38%
Female	89	$149,194	$1,044	$2,091	$4,546	$156,876	+5.15%
Total		$281,653	$1,952	$4,382	$8,470	$296,457	+5.26%

Source: http://www.hvsfinancial.com/PublicFiles/2017_Retirement_Health_Care_Costs_Data_Report_FINAL_6.13_V2.pdf

HealthView says that if you're at your end-of-life costs, and if you're a male, age 87 is your life expectancy. In addition, you're going to need approximately $139,000 for the last two years of your life. If you're a woman, your life expectancy is 89, and the cost of care is $156,000 for those last two years. And if you're a married couple, you need to have a budget of approximately $300,000, and that doesn't include chronic care. Plus, that's all today's dollars. So, when you estimate it in future dollars and include chronic care, that number is a little over $600,000. At this point, people stop me and ask, "Wait a minute, wait a minute, wait a minute. They're telling me that I need $600,000 for care. What if I don't have that much?"

Another question that should be asked is, "What if what I do have isn't completely mine?" One of the things I discuss in my book is what to do if the bulk of your savings is in an IRA, a 401(k), a 403b, or an annuity. You're probably familiar with these qualified plans. What do all these have in common? They're all tax-deferred plans.

We don't spend time talking about the costs of those deductions. Everybody is taught, "Take the deductions for your contributions while you're working. It will be great, and you could pass it to yourself when you're at retirement. You'll have lower income, everything will be phenomenal." But when you have the bulk of your net worth in one of those instruments, it's not really all your money. If you have $400,000 in a 401(k), you don't really have $400,000. The government has their hands in there, and they're going to get some of it. We don't know what that amount will be. It is based on how much you withdraw and what future tax rates are, but that's what these vehicles all have in common. People ask, "Wait, what if I get to retirement, and I don't have enough for these numbers? What if I get to retirement, and what I have is not all mine?

What am I going to do? What's the plan?" And I reply, "Well, there's really a simple and phenomenal solution that gets over-looked." But let me share a couple more highlights while we're talking about care.

$5,840

THE MEDIAN COST FOR
NURSE HEALTHCARE
IN ARIZONA FOR 2018

The above graphic is from skillednursing.org. They share cost-of-care for all types of ranges in retirement. The median cost for chronic care in the state of Arizona in 2018 was $5,840 per month Usually, everyone has a story of someone in their family who has had to receive some type of chronic care. My grandma needed eight years of skilled nursing, which was extremely expensive, and so we like to spend time focusing on what the costs-of-care amounts could be at the end of retirement. More importantly, we focus on how you can provide income for 30 to 40 years, and then have potentially million-dollar expenses covered from that same portfolio.

Medicare.gov tells you that Medicare does not cover long-term care, also called custodial care, and that's the only care for which you need to be solely responsible. For more information on nursing care or custodial care, visit nursingcare.org. So what they're saying is that Medicare doesn't pay for long-term care. If you go to longtermcare.gov, it says that long-term care may have an elimination period and may not completely cover you for chronic care. There's a gap there.

How does that gap get filled? How can you leverage tax reform to fill that gap? You can do so with life insurance. The exemption in Publication 525 grants the permission for tax-free distributions in this circumstance.

Let's sum up what we've covered so far. The government will not be able to keep their promises. Again, I'm not a fortune teller. I cannot see into the future, but I do read the information I'm being told to read. The government is saying they're not going to have enough. It's up to us. We need to step up and be responsible for our own situations, and that's why I'm writing this book. I want to be proactive and on the right side of history to share these solutions ahead of time.

We've learned what the cost of care is going to be in retirement; it is a significant event for which everyone should prepared. The difficulty of planning for care is having enough money to get you all the way through retirement without working so you can enjoy your golden years. Happy hour is every hour, you're going on cruises, and you're supposed to be having fun, right? But it's hard to know what you should budget for these care expenses. What do we do?

Segment a small percentage of your interest annually and set it off to the side to blow up a huge hot air balloon that will carry you off to the sunset.

Survey Question Four

4. HOW WELL HAVE YOU BUILT A PLAN FOR CARE INTO YOUR RETIREMENT INCLUDING FUTURE ADJUSTMENTS FOR INFLATION? TAKE A MINUTE TO ADDRESS THIS QUESTION. ONE IS, "I HAVEN'T PLANNED AT ALL," AND 10 IS, "I FEEL COMPLETELY CONFIDENT IN HAVING ALL COSTS PLANNED FOR, INCLUDING FUTURE ADJUSTMENTS FOR INFLATION."									
1	2	3	4	5	6		8	9	10

According to the AARP[4] "The $25 billion reduction would affect the payments that doctors, hospitals, and other health care providers receive for treating Medicare patients. Individual benefits would not change, nor would premiums, deductibles, or copays. But with so much less money going to providers, the cuts could have major impacts on patient access to health care— such as fewer physicians accepting Medicare patients."

"We're deeply concerned that the tax proposals being made will very directly affect the ability of Medicare to maintain services, and

---

4 The AARP Publication: www.aarp.org/politics-society/ advocacy/info-2017/senate-tax-Medicare-cuts-fd.hmtl

we do not think it is fair that older Americans who have paid into Medicare their entire working lives get stuck with the bill for a tax overhaul,"
— Christina Martin Frivida, AARP Director of Financial Security.

You already paid your Medicare premiums, and you already put money into the system. Why should you be taxed again when you need your own money? What is the solution? By implementing some tax diversification using life insurance, you can fix this! I mentioned this quote earlier in Chapter Two, and again, this book should be used more like a reference guide. Each chapter should be visited individually when needed. That is why you will find repetition throughout this book. I am layering important motifs, over and over, to drive my point home. It is important to revisit this quote because it is a crucial evaluation completed by a highly-reputable individual doing her best to directly communicate the likely shortfalls of Medicare.

Let's take one more second to answer the last survey question.

Survey Question Five

5. HOW WELL HAVE YOU DIVERSIFIED YOUR TAXABLE AND NON-TAXABLE BUCKETS CURRENTLY? ONE IS, "NOT DIVERSIFIED AT ALL," AND 10 IS "FEELING VERY DIVERSIFIED APPROPRIATELY FOR YOUR SITUATION." TAKE A MINUTE TO CIRCLE YOUR CHOICE.									
1	2	3	4	5	6		8	9	10

So why use a special type of life insurance to accomplish this tax diversification? It's instant estate, it's instant leverage, and it's money that you didn't have access to previously. It's also one of the only financial tools that has a privileged exemption in the tax code for a tax-free distribution.

Remember when I mentioned earlier about the challenges you will face when you get to retirement? You pretty much have what you have, and sometimes you don't have enough to budget for those costs for care. For most of us, what we have isn't all ours. Some of it belongs to the government, you just haven't taken it out yet, and neither have they. So, building up a big balloon in this special type of policy, if you qualify, will allow you to add instant estate to your portfolios, instant access to tax-free money for qualifying care costs. Essentially, somebody else pays to protect your net worth, so you don't have a negative net worth compounding effect of drawing your taxable money, not timing it correctly, and paying more than you need to, which reduces the total portfolio faster than managing the timing and size of your withdrawals each tax year. In other words, it is completely in your control to take advantage of tax reform by pulling out small controlled amounts of taxable money each year in this low environment and putting them into a tax-free benefit like life insurance with leveraged benefits for care costs. Again, this is not tax advice. Speak with your CPA regarding your situation prior to acting on this concept.

Using Life Insurance to Pay for Long-Term Care

Some life insurance policies include a feature that allows you to receive a tax-free advance on your life insurance death benefit while you are still alive. You may be required to pay an extra premium to add this feature to your life insurance policy, or the insurance company may include it in the policy for little to no cost.

With a website called longtermcare.gov, you would think they would be touting, like most people, the supremacy of long-term care insurance alone. Many people think, "I have a long-term care policy, I'm good." Well, look at what longtermcare.gov says about using life insurance to plan for long-term care in retirement. Some life insurance policies allow you to receive tax-free advances of the life insurance policy's death benefit while you're still alive. Again, people stop me and say, "Life insurance? That's crazy. That's only for when you die." However, this is a special type of rider that pays the death benefit while you're alive, completely tax-free, and in most scenarios, you can diversify 1-2% of just your gains and add 50 to 70% of your estate instantly if you need it for care. This is a very powerful tool offered as a solution from longtermcare.gov.

Publication 525

With all this talk about "tax advantaged" and "tax-free," let's talk about IRS.gov. Here it is! The publication from IRS.gov that makes this all possible—Publication 525. This the section of the code offers the provision to use life insurance for leverage to deploy tax-free access to benefits and allows you to take small amounts of money and transform them into large benefits payable to yourself tax-free for this event.

Remember, every Life Insurance company is different and you need to make sure you understand what qualifies as a claim to access the accelerated death benefit.

Publication 525 directly states what they refer to as taxable and non-taxable income. In regard to the accelerated death benefits of life insurance, Publication 525 says, "Certain amounts paid as accelerated death benefits under a life insurance contract, or life settlement before the insured's death are excluded from their income if the insured is terminally or chronically ill." So the IRS will actually allow you to diversify your portfolio to use a special type of policy and protect yourself with hundreds of thousands of tax-free dollars if you need money for care. Nobody is talking about it; it's a phenomenal strategy that's worked in practices all over the country, and it often flies under the radar.

Ok, I'm back. It's me the author, not the presenter. How did you like the presentation?

Is that enough proof for you? We're a couple of geeks! Before I segue into why this conversation flies under the radar and how our government has influenced our societal norms of financial education, let me share some feedback I've received. An audience member asked me a question at a speaking event, and it raised two key issues that I'd like to conclude with in case you have the same questions. This might shed light on what happens if you don't need the benefit for care. Also, it could explain how money moves through retirement using life insurance for people that have what is known as, "a tax-free withdrawal privilege."

Audience Member: "What if you never need care? What happens to the benefit?"

Daniel: "That is a really great question that comes up a lot. A couple of things happen. Remember that the care part comes from the death benefit (that's the leverage), but if you don't use that at all before you pass away, that benefit would be put tax-free into your estate or flow directly to your named beneficiary. If you have beneficiaries, or you have a trust or heirs, they will receive the entire lump sum, tax free, in case they need it for their own future healthcare costs or for anything else.

So that's another reason why I don't focus too heavily on care benefits riders alone (because I think there are risks of disappointment there). The death benefit is an important part of the need and solution. You could end up not needing to use the care. You could waste a bunch of money, and it's like your car insurance, you hope you never have to use it, but it would be nice to get something out of it. Now, there are return-of-premium products and products with death benefits, but I'm talking about a solution where you can lock in the premiums and have a guarantee that they will not increase when set up correctly."

Audience Member: "It can go directly to beneficiaries?"

Daniel: "Yes, if you never use it. So, say you plan for it when you're in your upper 80s, 90s, or even for centurions, in your hundreds, and you never use it. It will go right into your estate like all of your other assets, but it will go tax-free and probate-free with a named beneficiary. Plus, it's completely protected from predators and creditors accessing that money if set up and operated correctly after a certain period of time (some exceptions may apply. I am not a licensed attorney, CPA, or health insurance agent. This is all in Arizona, so please check with your local attorney for your state exemptions). Great question. Thank you. Anything else?"

Audience Member: "You said there were two ways."

Daniel: "Oh yes, thank you for reminding me. The other way is that some plans allow you to take income via a policy loan that must be correctly set up and maintained. This is a really popular strategy because many people want to supplement their income without increasing their taxes, so let's examine how that would work. Let's say you have only Social Security income right now, nothing else. Do you pay income tax?"

Audience Member: "No."

Daniel: "Correct, no income tax. There's a threshold, or a tax-free withdrawal privilege thanks to your standard deduction. So what if we diversified some of that money, using that tax-free withdrawal privilege, by moving it out of your fully-taxable accounts into this tax-free bucket?

Plus, now you're able to take Social Security, your tax-free withdrawal privilege which, depending on your age, your marital status, and how you file, can be different for everybody, but let's say it's $22,000. That's $12,000 from Social Security plus $10,000 of fully-taxable money that you were supposed to pay tax on. You now intentionally take it out of your qualified, pre-tax account, pay nothing, and then use a vehicle like life insurance to get tax-free income through loans that are again set up and maintained properly so that you don't lapse the policy or take a withdrawal and end up realizing income tax on your gains and potential penalties.

Now you can stack and build a tax-free retirement for yourself so you will have increasing income and decreased taxes. With a quick show of hands, who here would like to have higher income and lower taxes? That's another really popular use to help people protect themselves because if you have a tax-free retirement, it doesn't matter what future tax rates go to if your retirement is completely set up with the tax-free plans such as—Roth IRAs, HSAs, and potentially loans and accelerated death benefits from life insurance. That's a really great question to bring awareness and to clarify exactly how to implement this and what to expect."

I love that question. I included it because it allowed me to explain many of the intrinsic benefits of this strategy in a short amount of time. As the great National Speaker and Top of the Table legend Van Mueller says, "Life insurance is one dollar doing the job of many dollars." That is the power of using life insurance to your advantage—to leverage its proper use to guarantee the removal of risks when set up correctly. This is why it is crucial that you meet with the correct, trusted council. Van Mueller is the father of the tax-free withdrawal privilege strategy, a method of liberating hundreds of thousands of dollars from tax liability over a period of several years at potentially no cost.

I feel it is important to make sure you understand that there are many disciplines in finance. While a CPA or a Financial Advisor may also be licensed to sell life insurance, it doesn't mean they use it often enough to be the most knowledgeable or proficient. You want an agent who has the knowledge of these special types of life insurance policies, and that only comes from practice.

If you've been paying attention, you know I keep referring to these plans as "special types of life insurance." That is because not all polices are created equal. In fact, an agent who doesn't know what they're doing can be worse than a neglectful or uninformed advisor. It's like going to your primary care doctor and they say, "Oh yeah, I do heart surgeries occasionally on the weekends. I can help you with that procedure." What would you say? You'd say, "Heck no! I don't want to see the guy who does it occasionally and isn't a specialist. I want to see the heart surgeon who does nothing but ten surgeries a day and is booked out until next June! "

The same is true with this discipline. In fact, it is literally a life and death matter when you're talking about implementing life insurance into your portfolio—especially this type.

Okay, now that I got that disclaimer out there, what about the CPAs? Well, let's ask one. I asked Mark Renberg, a 37-year CPA veteran to tear apart my example above and provide his analysis. Let's take a look:

ASSUMPTIONS #1
Married Filing Jointly -
Gross Income $150,000 (Includes $100,000 Deferral)

GROSS INCOME	$150,000
SCH. A DEDUCTIONS	$85,000
MEDICAL EXPENSES	$100,000 less income limitations
TAXABLE	$65,000
TAX COMPUTATION	
10% BRACKET	$1,940
12% BRACKET	$5,472
TOTAL	$7,412
STATE TAX	
FIRST $21,202 AT 2.59%	$549
SECOND $31,798 AT 2.88%	$916
THIRD $12,000 AT 3.36%	$403
STATE INC TAX	$1,868

ASSUMPTIONS #2
Married Filing Jointly -
Gross Income $150,000 (Plus $100,000 Deferral)

GROSS INCOME	$250,000
SCH. A DEDUCTIONS	$85,000
MEDICAL EXPENSES	$100,000 less income limitations
TAXABLE	$175,000
TAX COMPUTATION	
10% BRACKET ($19,750)	$1,975
12% BRACKET ($60,500)	$7,260
22% BRACKET ($90,800)	$19,976
24% BRACKET ($3,950)	$948
$175,000 TOTAL	$30,159 Fed
STATE TAX	
FIRST $21,202 AT 2.59%	$549
SECOND $31,798 AT 2.88%	$916
THIRD $52,998 AT 3.36%	$1,781
FOURTH $69,002 AT 4.24%	$2,926
STATE INC TAX	$6,172

FUTURE ASSUMPTIONS #3

Married Filing Jointly - Gross Income $150,000, Plus $100,000 Deferral Scheduled for Medical Expenses Exceeding 25% AGI, Tax Rates Doubtful)

GROSS INCOME	$250,000
SCH. A DEDUCTIONS	$37,500
MEDICAL EXPENSES	$100,000 less income limitations

100,000 less deduction limitations computed as (100,000-[250,000 x .25]) = 100,000 less 62,500

TAX COMPUTATION $212,500	
20% BRACKET ($20,000)	$4,000
24% BRACKET ($65,000)	$15,600
44% BRACKET ($95,000)	$41,800
48% BRACKET ($32,500)	$15,600
TOTAL	$77,000
STATE TAX SIMILAR RATES TODAY	
FIRST $21,202 AT 2.59%	$549
SECOND $31,798 AT 2.88%	$916
THIRD $52,998 AT 3.36%	$1,781
FOURTH $144,002 AT 4.24%	$6,106
STATE INC TAX	$9,357

BASIC ASSUMPTIONS

DISTRIBUTION FROM DEFERRED INCOME ACCT. (401K) IS FULLY USED FOR MEDICAL EXPENSES - DEDUCTIBLE OVER THE 10% INCOME LIMITATION

MEDICAL EXPENSES DO NOT HAVE A DEDUCTIBILITY LIMIT AFTER 10% INCOME LIMITATION

FUTURE CONCERNS ON LARGE DISTRIBUTIONS FROM A DEFERRED INCOME ACCOUNTS:

1. TAX RATES IN THE FUTURE WILL IN ALL PROBABILITY INCREASE SIGNIFICANTLY

2. WE DON'T KNOW WHAT THE DEDUCTIBILITY WILL BE OF ITEMIZED DEDUCTIONS FOR MEDICAL EXPENSES WILL BE

3. AS INCOME GOES UP, IN PROBABLE TERMS, DEDUCTIONS WILL GO DOWN

This is for illustrative purposes only. Actual results may vary. This is not tax or investment advice. This is also not your representative of your individual situation. This is purely just an example for conversation purposes only. Please act on the recommendations of your advisers. This is not intended for you to act on in any way. This is an assumption of a possible scenario in the future.

Key Takeaways from CHAPTER FOUR: THE PROOF

Survey Question One

How comfortable are you with the strategies you discuss with your current advisors and tax professionals to take advantage of the new tax reform? One is not comfortable at all" and 10 is "extremely comfortable."

1 2 3 4 5 6 8 9 10

Survey Question Two

How important do you think that is to plan for budget cuts? On a scale, one represents "not at all," and 10 represents "extremely important to raise awareness and to be mindful of this budget cut."

1 2 3 4 5 6 8 9 10

Survey Question Three

Given the government's current liability, do you think taxes could be higher in the future? And here's the kicker that nobody asks, do you want to pay them? Rate yourself on a scale of one meaning "you feel like taxes will go down, and you're completely comfortable paying those future rates, whatever they are," to 10 meaning "you feel like taxes could skyrocket, and you're not comfortable with positioning your retirement to risk being taxed at a much higher rate."

1 2 3 4 5 6 8 9 10

Survey Question Four

How well have you built a plan for care into your retirement including future adjustments for inflation? Take a minute to address this question. One is, "I haven't planned at all," and 10 is, "I feel completely confident in having all costs planned for, including future adjustments for inflation."

1 2 3 4 5 6 8 9 10

Survey Question Five

How well have you diversified your taxes currently? One is, "not diversified at all," and 10 is "feeling very diversified appropriately for your situation." Take a minute to circle your choice.

1 2 3 4 5 6 8 9 10

- By building up a big balloon of this special type of policy, if you qualify, you can add instant estate to your portfolios and instant access to tax-free money for qualifying care costs.

- Essentially, somebody else pays to protect your net worth, so you don't have a negative net worth compounding effect of drawing your taxable money, not timing it correctly, and paying more than you need to, which reduces the total portfolio faster than managing the timing of your withdrawals each tax year.

- The IRS allows you to diversify your portfolio to use a special type of policy and protect yourself with hundreds of thousands of tax-free dollars if you need money for care. Not enough people are talking about it; it's a phenomenal strategy that's worked in practices all over the country, and it often flies under the radar.

- Publication 525 is the section of the code that offers the publication with the provision to use life insurance for leverage to deploy tax-free access to benefits, and they allow you to take small amounts of money and transform them into large benefits payable to yourself tax free for this event.

- Remember, every Life Insurance company is different and you need to make sure you understand what qualifies as a claim to access the accelerated death benefit.

- There are many disciplines in finance. While a CPA or a Financial Advisor may also be licensed to sell life insurance, it doesn't mean they use it often enough to be the most knowledgeable or proficient. You want an agent who has the knowledge of these special types of life insurance policies, and that only comes from practice.

Chapter Five: The Theory

"The problem is not that people are taxed too little. The problem is the government spends too much."

— Ronald Regan

"The crime of taxation is not in the taking it, it's in the way that it's spent."

— Will Rogers

"Why is our succession plans for widows with three children a Go Fund Me account with $17,000 funded?"

— Daniel Rondberg

"Women live longer, and they live with consequences, good or bad, of how much life insurance is on the man in their life. Show me a widow that is living poorly and a widow that is living well, and the difference is usually life insurance."

— Tom Hegna

"You mean to tell me they didn't have one life insurance agent in their lives that could do their job? Life insurance agents listen up. You suck. This happens way too often in our country. You are the only people who have the power to protect these people. You are the guardian angels of your communities. Stop letting the talking heads keep you down and go do your job!"

—Daniel Rondberg

Wow! Applause, it is an incredible rush of pure joy. It's not like I am a performer. I really have to be on and engage with my audience for people to clap afterward. I smiled, waved, and mouthed, "Thank you, thank you." The audience members gathered their materials and started to stand up and shuffle out the door. As the crowd began to thin out, I saw her. Instantly my heart sank. She was probably in her mid-seventies. She made eye contact as she slowly tried to maneuver against the flow of people, making her way towards me. She didn't have to say a word. I knew exactly what she was going to say. I've heard the same thing probably over 100 times at the end of almost all my live events. As she arrived directly in front of me, I heard that familiar echo.

"Hi. That was a great presentation. I really enjoyed it. I don't know if you can help me, though. My husband passed away. I only get his Social Security. I just moved in with my daughter. I'm running out of money. There was no life insurance, and I don't know what to do. Can you help me?"

This really is my reason for writing this book. I think about my wife and daughters being sweet 70, 80, 90 or even 100-year-old widows.

I want them to be comfortably sitting at home, or better yet, if able, traveling the world. I don't want them or anyone's loved ones repeating this narrative. This has to end. As the great Doctor Carl Hammershlag says, "Different endings to the same old stories." It's not exclusively a women's issue, but for every man I have telling me this story, I can show you nine women.

Now, if the man who predeceased her had this type of life insurance, the accelerated death benefit rider would provide tax-free liquidity while he was still alive to help protect her from spending down all the assets to take care of him. If he doesn't need care, that death benefit would be passed to her as a tax-free lump sum. She can then use this to create additional income or for her future care. This is why that when I hear men say, "I don't believe in life insurance," I want them and their wife to follow me down the street to the state-run nursing home to reexamine their beliefs together and weigh them against her ending up in that home.

Women are not helpless widows. They are strong and are earning more money than ever. In most houses, they run the show. Many households divide up tasks such as cooking, cleaning, and finances. Ideally, these things are done together, but often men will insist on controlling the money. Sometimes, these men also refuse to purchase life insurance because it's a "waste of money," or "they do not believe in it."

I am not here to judge or trounce on your beliefs. I am just the one here when your wife comes up to me after a seminar and tells me that she's lost her standard of living forever and, therefore, lost her choices and dignity. Most women will outlive their husbands because they typically marry older men and they have longer life expectancies. This is the actuarial data. If you don't believe in life insurance, and you run the finances, and you don't plan for your wife after your gone, remember that she's trusting you to have considered this as part of the responsibility of managing the money. What that really tells me is not that you "don't believe in life insurance." Sadly, the evidence shows you don't really care what happens to her after you're gone. Or, it could be it's too uncomfortable to deal with or you thought she'd be fine because you've made assumptions or you've received poor advice from your advisor. I have never said this to someone's face, and I don't feel very courageous for making such a bold statement in writing. If you're ready to burn my book right now because this is touching a nerve, please know that I genuinely write this with love and hope for you and your family. That this is the moment you embrace your mortality and the responsibility of ensuring that your spouse and or heirs are cared for.

If you are single and think only married suckers need life insurance, think again. While you may not have a spouse or direct heir that depends on your income, you need to insure just the same that if you have assets and don't want to end up as a ward of the state either because the cost of care is greater than those assets, that you look to this strategy as a possible consideration to accomplish this. Single people with no kids are among the highest demographic of people I personally help with this strategy.

Finally, if you are single with children that depend on you, mathematically, you are in one of the most difficult financial predicaments. Depending on your situation, you will need to provide for your children, alive or not.

You will have to save enough for retirement while doing so, retire and have the income to do it and then possibly need care after distributing 30 years of income from your savings all on your own. This is no easy task. Again, this is why you should leverage pennies for dollars to help you maximize every cent and take care of your mortality and morbidity risk for a fraction of your after tax wages.

These three demographics all must believe in at least learn enough about this strategy to decide whether it's a good idea. Fair enough? Great! Put down those matches and let's keep going. It's time to discuss my theory.

The theory is simple. If the government gets a percentage of your retirement account (your 401(k) or IRA), is there an incentive for them to see you do well? Absolutely! They have a vested interest in your performance. Stop and think about what has happened in our country for the last decade.

The government passes the Troubled Asset Relief Program (TARP) and pumps $757 billion into the market, accounting for approximately 50% of the bull run we have been on. In other words, the government spent a tremendous amount of money propping up the stock market. Simultaneously, they have taken on more debt than in any ten-year time span before.

Why? Again, there is a simple answer. Taking on debt isn't risky when you are also pumping up the largest population of retirees' accounts that you have a share in and when you decide how much you'll take and when you'll take it. With the amount of Baby Boomers retiring, they have more obligations to pay for than ever; the Baby Boomer retirement for the next ten years will be the first time in U.S. history when more money will be going out the door in the entitlement programs than coming into the Treasury through taxes. The government only has two choices, cut benefits or raise taxes. Do you see the path more clearly now? Is the iceberg appearing on the horizon? If they pump up everyone's fully-taxable retirement accounts like farmers do to animals, then there will be more there for the slaughter.

Let's do the math: there are approximately $10 trillion in tax-qualified accounts in the United States. If the government raise taxes by 10%, how much do they make on the withdrawals of that $10 trillion? The answer is it depends on too many variables to spend time on in this section, but you can see how it's a significant amount of money. Now, this is only on paper but if you don't think it's part of their accounting, why are they tracking it so closely? Likely, these accounts will grow and compound the forever taxable withdrawals that we will be trapped under. If you don't think they will do this, stop and think back to World War II, which was the last time we saw the national-debt to gross-domestic-product ratio this close, and the highest marginal tax rate was 92%. Compare that to today's 37% top rate. I'm not saying taxes will go up that high, but I'm saying you can see how much room there is when they do make that decision.

If you look back at the figure in Chapter Four, you can see the history of top marginal rates in our country were much higher. Remember the words of George Santayana, "History has a way of repeating itself. If we do not learn from it, we are doomed to repeat it!" If it is appropriate for your scenario, you can proactively take steps to pay taxes intentionally while they are on sale.

A good exercise to determine this would be to look at your current effective rate instead of your marginal rate. For example, if you are in the 12% marginal bracket (the highest percentage of income tax you pay on the last dollar you withdrawal), look at your effective rate (the average of the total tax you pay compared to your income). For instance, some people do not understand that our income tax code is progressive. This means it starts at 0% and then goes to 10%, then 12%, then 22%, and so on. Most people think if you're in the 12% bracket, you pay 12% tax on every dollar. This is not true. You pay 0% on the money that fills the 0% threshold, then 10% on the money that takes you through the 10% threshold, and 12% on every dollar that flows into the 12% range. Therefore, you did not pay 12% on every dollar. Depending on your scenario and income sources and amounts, you may average, or have an effective rate, of 4.5% (total tax paid on the total income). This is why I included the CPA analysis of my example conversation earlier.

Think of it like this: with everything you've learned so far, with all of the data you've gathered from this book, knowing that the government has out-of-control spending (that they used to have 94% tax rates), and that your future retirement account is the optimal choice for them to target since 50% of Americans have less than $25,000—knowing all of that—if you could purposely pay 4.5% tax today to never pay it again on the extra money you purposely withdraw, would you do it?

If your answer is no, stop reading; I have failed you. Please go down to the buffet and eat and drink until the iceberg tears through the deck into the dining hall as Uncle Sam puts ear plugs in your ears, covers your eyes with an eye mask, and massages your back while motioning to the remaining passengers to fill the lifeboats to capacity. Never mind that they are leaving you there and icy water is filling your shoes. If you said yes, then congratulations! You have taken the first steps toward purchasing your iceberg insurance policy, which is a beautiful, hot air balloon that can take you safely through your journey high above the perilous sea.

To conclude, figure out your effective rate. Ask yourself if you raise your taxable withdrawals by an additional amount that you would like to remove from those accounts, to pay the tax on, and reclassify to Roth or a post-tax option like life insurance so you can reduce your taxable liability, is that worth it? Remember the words of David McKnight, author of *The Power of Zero*, what are his two favorite tax brackets right now? 22% and 24%. Why? Because it's only a difference of 2%, and you can reclassify enormous amounts of money every year by maximizing the withdrawals in these brackets.

By the way, don't forget the words of Van Mueller, "If you are only in the 0% tax bracket, then you have a tax-free withdrawal privilege, meaning if you take the maximum taxable withdrawals you can and stay inside that threshold, you can potentially reclassify fully-taxable money and pay no income tax on it at all. You can do this for years and reclassify your entire taxable accounts that you received deductions on the contributions and were supposed to pay tax and pay nothing! Why would you not take advantage of that?"

Key Takeaways from CHAPTER FIVE: THE THEORY

The Troubled Asset Relief Program (TARP) pumped $757 billion into the market, accounting for approximately 50% of the bull run we have been on.

- In other words, the government spent a tremendous amount of money propping up the stock market.

- Simultaneously, the government has taken on more debt than in any ten-year timespan before.

- With the amount of Baby Boomers retiring, the government has more obligations to pay than ever. They have two choices: cut benefits or raise taxes.

Let's do the math.

- There are approximately $10 trillion in tax-qualified accounts in the United States.

- The government spent $757 billion through TARP passed in 2009 to stimulate the economy and inflate the market.

- World War II was the last time we saw the national-debt to gross-domestic-product ratio this close, and the highest marginal tax rate was 92%. Compare that to today's 37% top rate.

- Figure out your effective rate and ask yourself if you raise your taxable withdrawals by an additional amount that you would like to remove from those accounts, purposely pay the tax on, and reclassify to Roth or a post-tax account like life insurance so you can reduce your taxable liability, is that worth it?

- Remember the words of David McKnight author of *The Power of Zero*, what are his favorite two tax brackets right now? 22% and 24%. Because it's only a difference of 2%, and you can reclassify enormous amounts of money every year by maximizing the withdrawals in these brackets.

- By the way, don't forget the words of Van Mueller, "If you are only in the 0% tax bracket, then you have a tax-free withdrawal privilege, meaning if you take the maximum taxable withdrawals you can and stay inside that threshold, you can potentially reclassify fully-taxable money and pay no income tax on it at all. You can do this for years and reclassify your entire taxable accounts that you received deductions on the contributions and were supposed to pay tax and pay nothing! Why would you not take advantage of that?"

Chapter Six: The Interview

The following interview with Professor Laurence (Larry) Kotlikoff, one of the world's top 25 most influential economists, was completed in an hour-and-a-half on October 17, 2018. It has been condensed down to only the key points that the American people need to know.

Daniel: What presents a significant tax risk in our country for people who are approaching retirement?

Larry: The country's gone a little broke, and we can't cover these bills. And then, many are building up all these unfunded liabilities which are getting bigger each year as well. The total deficit this year will probably be about six trillion dollars.

The country's going to hell in a handbag in terms of how it's running the financial affairs. We're going to have to have higher taxes and lower benefits in the future. This is coming. All this raises the question of whether you want to have your money in a 401(k) or lose it.

What happened in Argentina can happen to our country. There is no country that is immune from running irresponsible fiscal policy.

Big, small, wealthy, and poor countries, they've all gotten into trouble over the years under irresponsible leadership and that's what we've got.

Daniel: What is the current fiscal gap to GDP today?

Larry: The absolute fiscal gap is about $220,000,000,000,000.

The fiscal gap is a comprehensive measure of our government's indebtedness. It is defined as the present value of all projected future expenditures, including servicing outstanding official federal debt, less the present value of all projected future tax and other receipts, and includes income accruing from the government's current ownership of financial assets.

According to recent International Monetary Fund (IMF) and Congressional Budget Office (CBO) projections, the U.S. fiscal gap is far larger than the official debt and is compounding very rapidly. The longer we wait to close the fiscal gap, the more difficult the adjustment will be for ourselves and for our children. This said, acknowledging the government's fiscal gap and deciding how to deal with it does not rule out productive government investments in infrastructure, education, research, or the environment, or in pro-growth tax reforms. This is why we have tried to pass the Inform Act.

Inform Act

The Intergenerational Financial Obligations Reform Act

The INFORM ACT requires the Congressional Budget Office (CBO), the General Accountability Office (GAO), and the Office of Management and Budget (OMB) to do fiscal gap accounting and generational accounting on an annual basis and, upon request by Congress, to use these accounting methods to evaluate major proposed changes in fiscal legislation.

Learn more about the Inform Act at https://theinformact.org

Our country has been playing "take as you go" on a massive scale for decades. The game is simple. Each generation takes from its children and leaves them to take from their children. Some of this shows up in officially reported debt. However, it's mostly hidden in the form of unfunded liabilities. The Inform Act is a bipartisan bill, which has been endorsed by thousands of economists, including 20 U.S. economics Nobel Laureates. It would require the Congressional Budget Office, the General Accountability Office, and the Office of Management and Budget to do fiscal gap and generational accounting annually and for all major fiscal reforms proposed by Congress.

Fiscal gap accounting puts all the country's obligations, including all its off-the-books obligations, on the books and compares them with the country's projected tax and other receipts. It would bring an effective end to deficit accounting, which has no basis in economic theory. Instead, what we measure as our government's deficit and, associated debt, is solely a figment of how we label government receipts and outlays, i.e., of the government's choice of fiscal language, not its fundamentals. Fiscal gap and generational accounting is now being done on a systematic basis by the European Union and has spread around the world. It's time for our government to make public, what it knows in private – our country is dead broke. With a fiscal gap north of $200 trillion, it represents a fiscal sword of Damocles for every young and future American

https://kotlikoff.net/fix-your-country/

So, it's about 10 years of GDP. Right now.

Daniel: In your recent film, you discussed how you have consistently put this legislation forward.

It gets close, and then it always gets stopped or suppressed. What doesn't the government want us to know about the fiscal gap?

Larry: The politicians have been hiding stuff off the books for years. They don't want us to know that they're running a Ponzi scheme. And I'm not sure that older people would want it revealed that they've been part of this. The adults would not want to recognize or be told that they've been part of a Ponzi scheme—that it kind of expropriates their children. But it's not just their children.

That's what people don't get. The burdens that are coming for the kids are too big for their kids to handle, so then they're going to have to cut back on benefits. And we're talking about a massive problem here that nobody is discussing publicly.

Daniel: Let's talk about retirement for a second because you really made it your mission with your study of personal finance behaviors. You're the President of Economic Security Planning, Inc., and I think a lot of people credit you with being one of the first people to really raise awareness to the Social Security maximization strategies. **If you were in meetings with these financial professionals, sitting across the table from the average American who saves in a 401(k), what would you share with them regarding tax considerations on those assets in the future?**

*Pay attention: this is the most important part of the interview. If you skimmed Professor Kotlikoff's resume in Chapter One, I just suggest you read it to get an appreciation for the simple fact that nobody has a better understanding of where our country is going

than Professor Kotlikoff. I bolded my last question. Read it again, and then read how Professor Kotlikoff responds.

Larry: Even without the uncertainty, a lot of people are not making plans to handle their finances. They look at their 401(k) that might have three or five hundred thousand dollars — they're not taking into account the taxes that are due on that money. They think they can spend it without a problem, but they have to pay taxes first. Just recognizing and understanding that this money is subject to taxation, and what that means for what you can spend now and how much more you need to save now, is important so you're not running out of money at the end of your days.

In addition, we have all the risks associated with taxes going up and benefits being cut that complicate the problem. So, one has to look at different scenarios. We've got to plan on how things turn out and the way they're projected — or at least the way the government says they're going turn out. And here's what I need to do to protect myself from the government lying to me, which is absolutely the case.

The government has been lying at this magnitude to the public about its finances for decades, and these problems are not problems that were made by the Democrats or the Republicans — it was made by both parties over time during Eisenhower and the postwar period. It's one thing to have social change programs, and I believe in them, but it's another to have an extremely poorly-designed and completely unproductive program so that you're forcing one generation to the next to pay for benefits for the old people. That's a Ponzi scheme. _So, we have to look at scenarios under which those retirement plans fail because the government is failing._

Daniel: What should you do if you're approaching retirement within five years, and you have almost 100% of your investible assets in qualified plans? How can individuals take control when the government fails?

Larry: Well, they must consider people maximizing their living standards that they accept possible alternatives. They're all contributing more right now to their accounts. They've chosen accounts that are pre-tax, so you pay your taxes up front and not down the road. It means deciding exactly when to take retirement account withdrawals so that you can minimize taxes. It requires being very smart about taking Social Security and making sure you get the maximum amount of benefits. It requires thinking about downsizing your home and moving to a state with no state taxes. It requires thinking about working longer—maybe working at a lower stress job but for a longer period of time.

Financially speaking, I don't think anybody in our country who isn't in great shape should be considering retiring. They should just work as long as possible. Things are that risky, and our longevity is such that any people are living to be age 100. About 300 million will be over 100 by the middle of the century, so the scenario is people over 100 are the fastest growing population in the country. Do they have a parent who did not die within the average life expectancy? Are they going to be on the hook to take care of that parent? They have to think about that as a special expense, that they're in the phase.

This requires planning, and thought, and analysis. It is not the time for quick and dirty, real fun calculations-based software that Wall Street designed to entice you into buying high-yield, risky mutual funds with very high fees—so that Wall Street gets rich and you become poor. Anybody facing the future must treat this as a very serious analytical problem and life problem. You can't just walk into old age without having thought it through.

Daniel: Let me ask one more question before we go because that brought up something interesting. Are you familiar with the data report that the independent non-profit HealthView services puts out every year?

Larry: No.

Daniel: They put out a report every year for the cost-of-care and retirement, and they project that if you're 65 years or older today, you will need approximately 90% of your Social Security check to cover healthcare costs and retirement. When I ask people about that report and the cost of pulling large lump sums out of their qualified plans, I've found that often there's not a plan for that. That's the focus of my book, and that's what I've been putting out there in terms of using life insurance as a tax diversification method so that they can access those dollars more effectively.

Larry: You're thinking about a whole life policy that would be throwing off income to help you cover your health insurance? Is that the idea?

Daniel: The idea is a policy with an "accelerated death benefit rider" that will allow you to access the death benefit tax-free for qualifying events. If you have a heart attack, a stroke, critical illness, chronic illness, terminal illness—or other type of qualifying events. My theory is that people who have saved the bulk of their measurable net worth in qualified dollars haven't given consideration to what if they need to use those dollars to cover these health problems and their large expenses.

Larry: End of life health expenses. It's life insurance like nursing home insurance. It's part of the co-joint policy. That's interesting. I wouldn't describe this as just life insurance per se because it's *really* more of a new type of policy that provides joint coverage. You cannot confuse insurance with savings, so you can't save up for insurable benefits. You can't save up to have your house burn down. You have to buy insurance. So that's one of the key points—making the distinction in the book between savings and insurance, that you can't save for cancer, operations, etc. As much money as we can put into an HSA, it's not going to matter—we'll still be broke if we don't have health insurance.

This approach to providing health protection, the HSA approach, is way off base. I'm friends with the guy who set up the whole system, John Goodman. I told him repeatedly, "This is not what was intended with health insurance. You need insurance." So yeah, we're on the same page, and now I see where you're coming from.

Sorry to pop in again, but this next part may be the greatest accomplishment of my career. Getting proof of concept on my methods from Professor Kotlikoff is like Michael Jordan telling me I have a champion-caliber game-winning jump shot.

Daniel: Thank you; I appreciate that. That's a huge compliment coming from you. My theory is that the average 401(k) balance is about $197,000. People are being told to plan for $280,000 in healthcare expenses and $400,000 for chronic illness. That math doesn't work. People are arriving to retirement without enough money, and they're arriving to retirement with something that's not theirs. What are they going to do?

Life insurance with a living benefit rider provides instant estate where somebody who maybe has $400,000 in a 401(k) can diversify a couple percent of their gains, and now instead of having $400,000 fully-taxable, they have $650,000 in benefits, and the first $250,000 comes out income-tax free for qualifying events that are really the high-risk scenarios where they would need to dip into those funds considerably.

Larry: You can't save your way through the future: you have to insure your way to deal with the potential health qualms. And the tax issues are interconnected. *__I think trying to use some life insurance, which doesn't sound exactly just like life insurance, would be important.__*

There you have it. Bone-chilling insight into our economy and the truth about how important it will be to take control of our retirement now while we can.

Key Takeaways from CHAPTER SIX: THE INTERVIEW

- **Daniel:** What presents such a significant tax risk in our country for people who are approaching retirement?

- **Larry:** So the country's going to hell in a handbag in terms of how it's running the financial affairs. We're going to have higher taxes and lower benefits in the future. This is coming and then that raises the question of whether you want to have your money in a 401(k) or lose it.

- **Daniel:** What is the current fiscal gap to GDP today?

- **Larry:** Well the absolute fiscal gap is about $220,000,000,000,000.

- **Daniel:** What don't they want us to know about the fiscal gap?

- **Larry:** The politicians have been hiding stuff off the books for years. They don't want us to know that they're running a Ponzi scheme...

- **Daniel:** If you were in meetings with these financial planners and agents sitting across the table from the average American who saves in a 401(k), what would you share with them regarding tax considerations on those assets in the future?

- **Larry:** So they think they can spend it without a problem, but they have to pay taxes first... And here's what I need to do to protect myself from the government lying to me, which is absolutely the case.

- **Daniel:** We have to look at scenarios under which those retirement plans fail because the government is failing.

- **Larry:** You cannot confuse insurance with savings, so you can't save up for insurable benefits. You can't save up to have your house burned down. You have to buy insurance.

- **Larry:** So, we have to look at scenarios under which those retirement plans fail because the government is failing.

- **Larry:** You can't save your way through the future: you have to insure your way to deal with the potential health qualms. And the tax issues are interconnected. I think trying to use some life Insurance, which doesn't sound exactly just like life insurance, would be important.

Chapter Seven: The Conclusion

"All financial vehicles are tools. They can be used poorly or properly. They are not good or bad. Therefore, any expert telling you to hate or love something should be immediately disqualified as a professional for making a recommendation based on their emotions or, in other words, based on their belief systems, which have governed the actions in their own lives and ultimately reflect how they get paid."
— Daniel Rondberg, 2018

"The government mandates almost all personal insurance now. How long until they decide to force us to buy life insurance, too? Then, if it's anything like how they handled health insurance, how long until the company benefits are reduced and premiums increase?
— Daniel Rondberg 2020

As I walk through the door of my client's home, familiar scenes comfort me. Silvia walks me to the table where we've sat many times before. We are laughing about a joke, we hug, and I sit down to discuss her recent windfall. Only this time, at her table, other than coffee and Rice Krispies squares, there is a full-page ad from the *Arizona Republic* laying out in front of us, and the title of the article is "ANNUITIES." Before I say a word, Silvia's face is overcome with a stern look—not typical for this most adorable, cheery 74-year-old lady.

She looks me dead in the eyes and says, "Daniel, I've known you for over eight years. I'm all ears for what you came here to talk about today but let me make one thing clear: I'm not buying an annuity. They are the worst and I hate them after reading this article."

I swallow a lump in my throat. I've never been reprimanded like this for something I didn't do, but I imagine the feelings of discomfort I was now experiencing was accurate for the situation.

I smiled, and said, "Well the good news is, I'm not here to sell you an annuity. I'm here to find out if I can be of assistance to you. Can you tell me what you need this new money to do for you?"

Okay. Pause. Quick background: Silvia just sold her rental property. She had been living with her daughter for years. Her house was always upside down and had been purchased by her late husband. Her daughter was helping her pay rent until it made sense to sell it. She has about $300 per month in expenses up and above the income she receives from her Social Security and small pension. She has a savings account with about $90,000, and now $40,000 from the proceeds of the sale of her home sale. Okay, and we're back...

Silvia unfolds with Panic. "I didn't net as much from the sale as I hoped, and I'm just distraught. I'm withdrawing from my principal every month. My money is getting smaller and smaller. I'm terrified I'm going to run out of money. I'm healthy as a horse. I could live to be 100! What should I do?"

I got a confused look that made my nose scrunch up a little. "Let me ask you, what if there was a tool that could provide you the additional $300 of monthly income you need, and that tool offered a guarantee that you would not outlive your money?" Her eyes perked up and she started to smile. I smiled, too, and continued, "And what if on top of all that, it guarantees you that it would provide that $300 every month for a long as you live, even if it is to age 100, and if you run out of money, the checks never stopped? It would be like your pension and Social Security. You'd have guaranteed income for as long as you live. Plus, if you became sick and disabled, and your doctor wrote a letter certifying that you could no longer perform two out of the six activities of daily living, then your income would double, accelerating those payments to protect you from drawing down even more from your savings during that stressful time. What if it could do something like that?"

Her eyes swelled with hope. She said, "Daniel that would be perfect. That is exactly what I need, but where am I going to find a kind of tool that can provide something like that?"

My jaw literally dropped. It was in that moment I realized the real reason more people don't have the proper tools to protect themselves and why no one is having this conversation is that the trusted media and advertisements tell us something is bad or a rip off enough times, and we start to believe it.

In my practice, I never make a recommendation without the appropriate basis and only if warranted from my client. Allow me clearly delineate the following statement from being a recommendation.

When financial experts say life insurance is a terrible investment, they are right. Life insurance is for removing risk. We would all be a lot better off, and the radio waves would be a more peaceful place, if we stop trying to use only savings to manage key retirement risks. These products were built to manage these risks. Like professor Kotlikoff said earlier, you wouldn't start a savings account in case your house burnt down—you buy insurance. We need to stop spending so much time trying to convince people life insurance is a good or bad investment. Use the right tool for the right job, and you'll get a better result. Anyone telling you otherwise is selling you the wrong product.

Oh, and the end of the story is Silvia walked me to my car with a plate of fresh-baked Rice Krispies squares and genuinely thanked me from the bottom of her heart for helping her complete an application for an annuity.

There are so many "Financial Pundits" out there that say, "This is bad," or, "This is great." When did the biggest marketer with the biggest advertisement budget become the best source for financial education? We need to stop getting our financial education from people trying to sell us things. Let me be clear: while I am currently an agent, I did not write this book to advertise for the sale of insurance in my own practice. I have been the number one life producer at my agency for the last four years. I am currently writing as much business as I can handle responsibly. I wrote this book so that in communities across America that I have zero reach or impact in can have this message, and hopefully work with their trusted and skilled agents to help them address their own situations appropriately.

Again, life insurance in not the answer for everyone. It is also not the "best" or only answer. Everyone's situation is unique. I just want this book to serve as an equalizer to offer the most information and shed light on potentially-threatening, unexamined areas of our economy and the risk it presents for retirees today. Before I get letters from angry readers who want to argue or debate with me, I want to say this again as clearly as possible. I am not for or against life insurance as a product. However, I am very, very, very against someone's grandma running out of money, suffering in the later stages of life, living with no joy and immense anxiety because she did not have the right information and tools for her situation because some sales person at a free dinner seminar said life insurance is a rip off. I am very against this broken record. However, the product itself is not good or bad. It is only a tool and it performs a job. Saying life insurance is bad is like saying a hammer is bad when you're using it to saw a board in half.

It is supposed to be happily ever, after not curl up in a shared 10x10 state-run facility and say things like, "It would just be better for everyone if I died." I will not stand for that any longer. I want grandmas and grandpas in this country to have their happily ever after, too. They deserve it. By the way, long before all these experts, coaching programs, and podcasts, we did not have a retirement crisis and people running out of money. If all these people who tell you that life insurance is bad are accurate in saying so, I invite them to join me after my workshop to look in that sweet little widow's terrified eyes as she tells me with regret that her husband cancelled their life insurance policy to save money. That is where my heart is. We need to do a better job of considering all the information and facts before we adopt our beliefs. That is the only way we'll have a more informed consumer. We need our country to become more informed so we can make good decisions and not be swayed by blanket advise.

Do you know the first thing they taught me on day one at investment training class at J.P. Morgan? *There is no such thing as blanket advice.* Every single person has a different circumstance, and only when you completely evaluate their individual needs can you serve them properly. You can see how harmful the alternative can be. Someone was almost gravely harmed by information that was clearly not intended for her. Please, let this message serve you. This book is not based on my opinion. Hopefully by now, you can see the great lengths I've gone to bring you unbiased education to support this philosophy. All "risk" means is the possibility that something can go wrong. Remember Murphy's Law: "If something can go wrong..." you finish the rest. So, if you leave risk in your life, you're inviting in the possibility of something going wrong. Life insurance neutralizes risks. Therefore, when used properly, it is nothing more than a tool to eliminate the risk or possibility of something going wrong. Even better, it's one of the only tools that provides a contractual guarantee that nothing will go wrong because it takes care of you and your family even when you are not there to do it yourself. What other tool provides guarantees like that?

Now, you may be asking yourself, "Daniel, if this is such a simple and obvious problem, why is no one having this conversation?" Sadly, there are two answers, and neither bode well for the financial community at large. Both financial advisors and insurance agents are to blame for the lack of awareness we raise to this key retirement risk, simply because they are the ones responsible for managing it. To cut them a little slack, and to be as transparent as possible, life insurance can be one of the most difficult conversations to have with somebody. If you aren't a practitioner, the process can be overwhelming. It does require dedication and years of practice to really align it with your business. Sadly, many agents go out of business or quit before they can become successful at helping people with it.

There are two reasons why the advisors and agents that do make it aren't currently doing a better job:

1.   You need to look at who you're working with in two ways.

    a.   What is their financial discipline?

    b.   How do they get paid?

That is where some financial advisors have blood on their hands. Now on to the agents.

2.   You need to look at the culture of insurance professionals in this country.

I travel around the country and I get to meet a lot of insurance agents. I can see why some financial experts hate us. They would rather tell you a million and one reasons why something won't work because they are stuck in their own beliefs than try something new for their client. Unfortunately, here is the truth: there are people in this business who care more about their check then their clients, and they are nothing more than salespeople. Now, this is true in every financial discipline, but I'm purposefully shining a light on insurance agents. The reason being is, they are the discipline responsible for educating themselves and increasing their skill levels through private practice to the point where they can intelligently and proficiently help people with this challenge. They are also the only people in America with a license to execute these strategies.

Just a quick side note. There are a lot of online life insurance brokers now that can help you easily buy term insurance. Term insurance is only designed to cover you for a term, one period of time. Then, the policy either lapses or is converted to another policy that increases your premiums until you drop it all together. Again, term is not bad, and neither are online brokers. If you use the wrong tool for the job, you may not get the result you desired. This strategy is designed to be completed by a dedicated individual who you trust and already work with because they understand your situation and will ask the right questions to help determine if this is suitable.

Sadly, most agents will not put in the extra time to learn and master this crucial area of our craft. I know this because I stand in front of hundreds of them screaming and proving to them the importance and urgency needed. I even encourage them to steal all my materials and make it their own. Unanimously, I get a room full of head-nodding, complimentary, fired-up agents, but when I follow up, they have not followed the process to begin making a difference in people's lives.

However, most is not all. This is where I pride myself on raising the bar and distinguishing myself from the majority. By having a better conversation, there can be better results. It is not only my job to have this conversation with clients but agents as well, and as I work constantly to improve the culture of this discipline, I have found like-minded individuals within the community. If your advisor or agent put this book in your hands, it's because they understand the severity and care enough about you to have a difficult conversation with you, but rest assured, they have access to all my training, strategies, and even the exact companies I use for my own personal policies.

If your current advisory team did not put this book in your hands, do not be discouraged. They may not know about it. Or they may have a plan to address this. I encourage you to gather them together for a meeting in the immediate future and ask them to draw out your situation as I did in the example above. Ask them the following:

1. If I need to use my IRA, 401(k), etc. to pay for the current, expected chronic illness costs in future dollars, how much will that cost me including what I'll pay in taxes?

2. What strategies have we currently implemented to take advantage of this tax reform to restructure my fully-taxable accounts to give me tax-free access to money in the future?

3. Why am I not using my current, tax-free withdrawal or tax-advantaged withdrawal privilege every calendar year to help prepare for future healthcare costs?

   (If you don't have one,) then ask: What is the cost for reclassifying my taxable accounts into tax-free solutions using my effective and marginal tax rates?

4. What is our current exit strategy of these tax-deferred accounts other than death, donation, or paying the taxes?

If your current team cannot answer these questions instantly, that may be your indication that they are managing your portfolio to the best of their discipline's ability, but you may want to find someone who is the master of this financial discipline to help you set this up correctly.

If you would like a copy of these questions emailed to you, please email info@ theretirementresearchfoundation.com. The Retirement Research Foundation is a FREE educational resource that does not sell financial products, have clients, or make recommendations.

The final challenge to verify my message is simple. If you have any brokerage account at all, go to that brokerage's website, and find the section that talks about approximately how much you'll need for long-term care. Almost every major company has a recommended amount and describes the risk, and so the question becomes, "If this is what the company is recommending, I have set aside for this risk, why don't I have a current plan for this?" If you've been working with these professionals for a long time, and this is coming to light now, then the evidence suggests your planning may not be complete, and this is where this strategy fits in. Especially since the brokerage holding your money is telling you what they recommend. Here are a few popular examples for you to reference:

1. Charles Schwab: $503,100 (nursing home costs in 20 years) – https://www.schwab.com/public/file/P-8003542/ MKT53606-02_Long-term_Care_Insurance.pdf

2. Fidelity: $257,328 (average semi-private room for three years) – https://www.fidelity.com/viewpoints/personal-finance/long-term-care-costs-options

3. Edward Jones: $200,000 (in today's dollars) – https://www.edwardjones.com/preparing-for-your-future/unexpected/medicare.html

4. J.P. Morgan: $107,500 (approximate average median semi private room cost per year) – https://am.jpmorgan.com/us/en/asset- management/gim/per/ insights/guide-to-retirement/ retirement-discussions/know-what-to-expect-with-health- care-costs

5. Merrill Lynch: $97,000 (approximate median private room nursing home cost per year) – https://www.merrilledge.com/article/understanding-long-term-care-insurance

Thank you so much for reading my book. It's a dream come true to see my calling in life in words, and I cannot describe the joy I get from sharing it with you. I believe that we can all make a difference in this world. This is my avenue to spread some good and leave the world a little better than I found it. I'm blessed to have found my life's purpose so early on. I love this industry and the people who care about people. Please let me share a final thought with you. It's a poem that my mentor Van Mueller shared with me, and I read it with tears in my eyes at the end of every presentation I give.

I am a piece of paper. But even more I am an idea, I am a promise.

I help people see visions, dream dreams, and achieve economic immortality.

I am an education for the children, I am savings, I am also property that increases in value from year to year.

I lend money when you need it most, with no questions asked.

I pay off mortgages so that the family can remain together in their own home.

Assure fathers and mothers the daring to live and the moral right to die.

I create, manage, and distribute property.

I guarantee the continuity of business. I protect the jobs of employees. I conserve the employer's investment.

I am a tangible piece of evidence that a man or woman is a good spouse and parent.

I am a declaration of financial independence, a charter of economic freedom. I am the difference between an "old man" and an "elderly gentlemen." I am the only thing that a father or mother can buy on the installment plan and the survivor doesn't have to finish paying for.

I am a certificate of character, an evidence of good citizenship, an unimpeachable title to the right of self-government.

I am protected by laws that prevent creditors from accessing the money I give to your loved ones.

I bring dignity, peace of mind and security to the latter years of life.

I am the great social compact that merges the individual into the mass and places behind the frailty of human beings, standing alone, the immeasurable strength of human beings, standing together.

I supply investment capital that makes the smoke go up the chimneys, wheels turn, and motors hum.

I guarantee that there will always be Christmas, with tinsel, a happy fireside, and the laughter of children even though a bread-winner parent is no longer there.

I am the guardian angel of your home. I am your life insurance policy!

Key Takeaways from CHAPTER SEVEN: THE CONCLUSION

- Use the right tool for the right job, and you'll get a better result. Anyone telling you otherwise is selling you the wrong product.

- When did the biggest marketer with the biggest advertisement budget become the best source for financial education? We need to stop getting our financial education from people trying to sell us things.

- The product itself is not good or bad. It is only a tool and it performs a job. Saying life insurance is bad is like saying a hammer is bad when you're using it to saw a board in half.

- We need to do a better job of considering all the information and facts before we adopt our beliefs. That is the only way we'll have a more informed consumer. We need our country to become more informed so we can make good decisions and not be swayed by blanket advise.

- All "risk" means is the possibility that something can go wrong. If you leave risk in your life, you're inviting the possibility of something going wrong. Remember Murphy's Law, "If something can go wrong…" You finish the rest. All Life insurance does is neutralize risks. When used properly, it is nothing more than a tool to eliminate the risk or possibility of something going wrong.

- Both financial advisors and insurance agents are to blame for the lack of awareness to this key retirement risk, simply because they are the ones responsible for managing it.

- There are two reasons why the advisors and agents that do make it aren't currently doing a better job.

    a. Their financial discipline and how they are paid

    b. The culture of insurance professionals in this country.

By having a better conversation, I believe there can be better results.

- If your current advisory team did not put this book in your hands, I encourage you to gather them together for a meeting in the immediate future and ask them to draw out your situation as I did in the example above. Ask them the following:

1. If I need to use my IRA, 401(k), etc. to pay for the current, expected chronic illness costs in future dollars, how much will that cost me including what I'll pay in taxes?

2. What strategies have we currently implemented to take advantage of this tax reform to restructure my fully-taxable accounts to give me tax-free access to money in the future?

3. Why am I not using my current, tax-free withdrawal privilege every calendar year to help plan for future healthcare costs?

4. If you don't have one, then ask: What is the cost for reclassifying my taxable accounts into tax-free solutions using my effective and marginal tax rates?

5. What is our current exit strategy of these tax-deferred accounts other than death, donation, or paying the taxes?

If you would like a copy of these questions emailed to you please email: info@theretirementresearchfoundation.com.

Bonuses

"Tax diversification gives you one thing — control. You get to choose how you pay your taxes not the government."
—Daniel Rondberg

Have you ever heard the expression, *Do you want to know how the watch works or what time it is?*

In the following bonus sections, I am not only going to show you how the watch works, I am going to give you the holy grail of watches. A watch so powerful that it will allow you to travel back in time from your future retirement to hand yourself this book. This is your Biff handing you *The Sports Almanac* moment. Sadly, you learned about these bonus strategies too late to deploy. So you had to travel back and give yourself these tools in order to have the retirement you'll need to properly navigate the tax environment of the future. You not only gave yourself this book with the bonus sections, but included a note:

Dear Past Me,

The future is amazing. President Taylor Swift is doing a nice job leading the country. The only thing we didn't plan for was how much higher taxes are. Read the sections below and go to your current team of professionals to assist you in accomplishing what is appropriate. Take care.

Love,
Future You

P.S. Lose the ducky lips in all your photos. You don't enjoy them as much looking back later.

Ok, so future you did not visit me to write this book and deliver it to you. That last section was just for me. I enjoy the challenge of trying to make someone smile while reading a book about tax diversification and interpreting tax codes that describe vehicles that leverage qualified care expenses in retirement. Wow, that is a mouthful.

In the rest of the book, I will be giving away my best strategies for you in the remaining time we have together. These next sections are very much how the watch works. Most financial professionals don't know what I'm talking about when I share these strategies with them.

Because I am going to be very detailed here, I must include a pretty hefty disclaimer before I jump in. Also, I really hate when someone who specializes in a certain field uses industry-specific jargon that I may not fully understand when talking to me. I find it almost disrespectful. That's why I will do my best to describe this in general terms, but there will be specific explanations in which I will be using some industry-specific terminology. Again, it is so important for you to work with the right professional that can help you decipher and deploy the right strategy for you.

Disclaimer: All life insurance must meet the suitability guidelines and all insurance agents must adhere to their governing department of insurance guidelines to ensure that all sales are suitable. I am not a tax expert or CPA and I am not predicting taxes will go up. I am just sharing the research from tax experts. While life insurance is never purchased as an investment, it should not be purchases with the expectation of getting a return you don't buy life insurance strictly for any purpose other than the death benefit but there is no reason you can't take a loan from the cash value against death benefit. Every strategy, scenario and example are hypothetical. A 10% IRS penalty may apply to withdrawals prior to age 59 ½. Any reference to an insurance policy guaranty is referencing the contractual guarantees This is general insurance information this Is not a specific recommendation and should not be applied to any ones individual situation. I am not a CPA Attorney or Advisor. Speak with your team of advisors and council. I am not endorsing or discussing any specific product of any one company. I am also not making any guaranty that these strategies will work for you. Guarantees rely on the financial strength and claims-paying ability of the issuing insurer Any application must be complete by qualified licensed professional that you decide to work with. Not all products are available in all states. Surrender charges may apply to withdrawals during the surrender period. These products are not guaranteed by any bank or credit union and are not insured by the FDIC or any other federal government agency.

Bonus Number One

For the pre-retiree ages 20-50. Refinance your taxable and after-tax savings to a potentially tax-free retirement.

As a sincere thank you for reading my book, I want to share a powerful strategy for people who are not yet in retirement but are preparing for it. It could take an entire book to share all the information about this strategy, however, I can share with you this simple concept.

If you read this book, and your mind and heart are on future generations, and, if you consider today's problems, what will it be like for them someday? Will there even be Social Security and Medicare? Will only the ultra-wealthy afford healthcare? Will they be able to retire or have any quality of life? Do not worry, they also have a powerful tool at their disposal because they have time, and time plus money equals literal miracles.

"Compound interest is the eighth wonder of the world. He who understands it, earns it... he who doesn't... pays it."
— Albert Einstein

The simplest way to explain this strategy is that it's almost the opposite of the life insurance scenario outlined in this book in which we create the maximum leverage with the least amount of money. Since this is a preretirement scenario, we are going to do the opposite. We want to structure a special type of life insurance policy and contribute the maximum allowed while the IRS still permits us to call it life insurance. This creates a different type of leverage.

It allows someone with a qualified plan such as a 401(k), 403(b), or an IRA to also have this type of life insurance. The end goal is to be able to reclassify the entire qualified plan and have a completely tax-free retirement. Now, I present another disclaimer: This is not advice. The basis of this working depends on your income, savings, objectives, goals, experience, health, time horizon, financial situation, risk capacity, and a booklet of disclosures that would be appropriate when the structure is created. However, for discussion purposes, allow me to just demonstrate the general concept.

First, I need a volunteer. Just kidding. See, my jokes land! First, I need to lay the groundwork. Let's say you take a loan from a bank to buy a car. (Now I know what you're thinking. See, isn't it great to see how well we've gotten to know each other throughout this book?) You're thinking, *Daniel, why the heck are you telling me about a car loan?* I promise if you stick with me until the end, you will have the greatest light bulb moment! It will all be worth it.

You take a loan to buy the car and what happens? You make principal and interest payments to that bank until the loan is satisfied. You get the car and the bank gets all the principal and interest back. Right? Pretty easy, so far. Almost too obvious. Let's talk about that loan for one second. What happens if you don't make a payment? The bank will repossess your car. Why? Because of something called an *amortization schedule.*

Amortization refers to the process of paying off a debt over time through regular payments. An amortization schedule is a table detailing each periodic payment on an amortizing loan, as generated by an amortization calculator.

Again, this is obvious. All loans work this way. Did you know that you can loan money to yourself from your life insurance policy? However, this loan doesn't come with an amortization schedule. Why would that be? Well, it's simple. The life insurance company doesn't care if you pay the loan back or not, because if you never pay it back, they'll just subtract the balance plus interest from your death benefit. Again, it comes with a large death benefit, which is always worth more than the money you have in the policy. That's the leverage, so who really cares. You didn't buy the life insurance policy for the death benefit claim upon your passing. While life insurance is never purchased as an investment, and you don't buy life insurance strictly for any purpose other than the death benefit, there is no reason you can't take a loan against the cash value of the death benefit.

Let's apply this principle to our car example. Say you buy the same car with a loan from your life insurance policy. You make a few payments to yourself that go back into your policy. Then, you stop making payment.

You aren't required to make any more payments, and the life insurance company will pay off the loan plus interest when you die. "Ok great, Daniel, but we aren't trying to buy a car. We are talking about a retirement crisis." Hold on... we're almost there.

Here's where it gets crazy. What happens if you applied this lending principal to your retirement accounts? Here's a simple example.

Let's say you have $250,000 in 401(k) assets. You have saved properly and fully funded everything, putting approximately $100,000 into the special type of max-funded insurance policy.

So, your assets look like this:

$250,000 401(k) fully taxable.

$100,000 Life Insurance Tax-free death benefit, potentially accelerated death benefits, and potential loans from the policy.

What is the only current exit strategy for these retirement accounts? You can pay the taxes, you can give it away, or you can die. None of which sound very appealing.

Let's look at paying the taxes, but let's do it with Roth conversations. Doing this allows you to pay all the tax at one time but going forward, you now have a Roth IRA instead of a 401(k) or Traditional IRA, meaning you went from fully-taxable accounts to tax-free accounts. Again, I want to be clear, this is not tax advice, and there are many stipulations and rules that must be followed. That is why you need to speak with the right agent and CPA when establishing this strategy.

Ok, where were we? For five years, you convert $50,000 of the $250,000 into a Roth IRA. Let's say you a pay 24% federal rate on the $50,000 conversion ($12,000).

If you do that for five years, you will pay approximately $60,000 in taxes, but you'll end up with $250,000 in a tax-free Roth IRA. If you don't withhold any taxes and you just convert the full $250,000, where does the $12,000 tax payment for each of those five years come from?

Here's where your special lending privilege life insurance policy comes into play. You take five $12,000 loans from the policy, one each year for five years, for each subsequent tax payment to the IRS for each annual $50,000 Roth conversion, knowing you have no intention of paying the policy back. Instead, you let the life insurance death benefit pay off the loans (your tax bill) plus interest when you die. If structured properly and if the policy performs, your cash value will not only grow back, but so will your death benefit. This depends on the type of policy and many other factors, but it is possible. It should not be expected but it can happen.

Your entire portfolio can move forward with potential tax-free access with the Roth IRA and life insurance policy loans, if set up and exercised properly. Compound those now tax-free returns compared to after-tax and pre-returns and you tell me what the better move was over potentially 40 years of compound interest.

If taxes are raised significantly, you are completely protected from future tax hikes, resulting in a lower net retirement income since you paid the taxes today. Your retirement income will always be protected. You paid your taxes, so the IRS is happy, and because you did it at one of the lowest tax rates we've ever seen, you're happy. The life insurance company gets their money back by paying less death benefits to your beneficiary when you die, so they are happy. It's a win-win-win. Just remember, policy withdrawals and surrenders do not offer potentially tax-free access. It must be the correct type of policy loan against the tax-free death benefit. This is important. It is also important to note that Qualified plans and life insurance have potential withdrawal penalties under age 59½. Life insurance loans set up and maintained properly are not subject to pre 59½ penalties unless structured as a modified endowment contract.

Bonus Number Two

The Modified Endowment Contract (MEC)! How to add Life Insurance and Accelerated Death Benefits to your existing savings without paying expensive monthly premiums.

The Modified Endowment Contract or MEC tool is underused and under-evaluated when talking about retirement income. A MEC allows you to build in some potential life insurance coverage in retirement, and for some people, life insurance coverage serves a purpose in retirement. Many people say, *Well, how can I afford life insurance when I'm in my sixties, seventies, or my eighties? Isn't that cost prohibitive?* In certain cases, life insurance can be a valuable tool to help you identify and evaluate the best income choice. If you're looking to maximize your social security, or if you have a pension or annuity choice to make, you always want to select the best option.

Do I delay benefits? Do I take the higher income? Do I take the lower joint income if I'm married? Which strategy do I choose? How can I maximize that income?

If you need to protect a spouse or an heir, life insurance can play a key role. The amount of life insurance you have can make a big difference in which income option you choose as part of the evaluation process. Some people ask, *"Isn't that cost prohibitive? If I pay an expensive premium every year, why would I fork out a bunch of money for a life insurance policy, a strategy that will actually lower my income by paying premiums, just to get a higher income on an annuity or a pension if I'm lucky enough to have one?"*

Well, in the traditional sense, I would agree with you. Maybe the premium payment doesn't make sense if you're trying to maximize your income or protect a surviving spouse or an heir. Yet, we're talking about ways to build in life insurance benefits without having to pay a big annual premium. This is where the MEC comes into play. A MEC is a single-pay life insurance policy in which the premiums are all paid upfront with no additional premiums due. Many ask why it's called a modified endowment contract and not life insurance. With an MEC, you're funding the policy all at once, since the IRS takes away its ability to fund tax-free loans from the cash value or take tax-free loans pre 59½ as I mentioned earlier. Some life insurance policies, when structured as non-MEC, allow you to take loans tax-free from the policy when set up and maintained correctly. When you purposely make it a modified endowment contract, you void the tax-free loan privilege. Not to worry! I'm going to explain why retirees may have savings in a bank account for easy access in case of an emergency. Retirees are the greatest savings generation still on planet earth. They are good stewards of their money, they're great savers, and they've learned to live on the fixed income they have.

That same senior savings account sometimes builds up over time to much more than is needed for a liquid reserve fund. Some retirees have built savings up to $200,000, and now they're uncomfortable. This money is earning practically nothing sitting in the savings account, but it needs to be kept safe, and liquid. What do you do in that scenario, and how can this help boost your retirement income? A retiree in their sixties or seventies with $200,000 in savings can take $100,000 and put it in a modified endowment contract with a life insurance company. It comes with a cash value contractual guarantee, and there are also certain riders you can put on the policy to make that cash value liquid from day one.

You get the contractual guarantee of your principal and an interest rate from the life insurance company and you get the guaranteed liquidity with the rider from the company. This can create safety and liquidity which was the original goal of the savings account.

If you put $100,000 in the MEC, it might come with $150,000 or 200,000 of tax-free life insurance, so now you start to see the benefits. You put $100,000 that was just sitting in the bank into a modified endowment contract, and now it's worth 200,000 with $100,000 of tax-free life insurance as supplemental coverage that comes with the MEC. Next, when you go to evaluate your annuity choice, your pension choice, your social security choice, you have that death benefit to protect your spouse or heir as part of the consideration

If you can't perform certain activities of daily living, you go into a nursing home, or you become terminally ill, that benefit can pay out tax-free while you're alive, making it a living benefit. Once again, you are prevented from spending down your assets or draining all of your excess income to take care of one spouse, leaving the other spouse high and dry. This can come in the form of an accelerated death benefit rider as I previously discussed. You can use the insurance company's money to help pay for some of those costs, tax free. While a modified endowment contract has lost its tax-free privilege from loans of the cash value, the death benefit and living benefits still come out tax free if you need that accelerated benefit or if you pass away.

Some MECs, when specifically designed for care costs such as a combined benefits product, as I'll elaborate on in bonus number three, can even have an increasing benefit. A couple with $100,000 can take out two MECs (one for each individual) and end up with more than $300,000 of benefits each! You can see how meaningful the results can be. And, if they change their mind, they have a contractual guarantee that not only do they never have to contribute more money, but they can cash it in and take all their money back out.

This way, hacking into some of the supplemental life insurance coverage without having to fork over premiums in the forms of annual or monthly deductions form your income rather your excess savings, can be an efficient way to build in benefits. People ask me all the time, "Why would I leave my money sitting here in a savings account practically earning nothing not getting paid any benefits for it when I could move it to a modified endowment contract and get that extra benefit?" And so in some cases, that makes sense. It's not right for every single person and it's not right for every single dollar, but an MEC certainly serves its purpose and should deserve a role in your consideration process when you're in retirement if it makes sense for you. All I'm saying is it goes underutilized and undervalued and not many people know about this really, really great way to hack in some extra benefits on money that you want to keep sitting there safe and liquid.

The reason I say it is underutilized and undervalued is in my travels around the country, less then 5% of the agents I spoke with were using MECs. Truthfully, they told me in a survey that they focused on the absence of the potentially tax-free withdrawal privilege as a disqualifier. It is always so important to focus on what the goal of the money is. Remember, if it is to build-in benefits and the cash value grows comparable to the interest earned on a savings account, then it's not a very relevant disqualification.

Now there's another strategy for it that I'm going to throw in as a quick bonus that was made popular by the economist Tom Hegna. He talks about how people try to build their estate plan where they maybe keep $100,000 in an account over here for their three kids, as an example. They want to leave this $100,000 alone so it can go to their heirs. Well, that's inefficient. In that scenario, you're taking $100,000 to leave $100,000. Why would you do that when you could take $50,000 to purchase a MEC that's worth $100,000 if you die, and then you can spend the other $50,000 or use it for retirement income or a trip or whatever it is you need, maybe extra money you want to save or use $100,000 to inherit them $150,000.

That's a better way to structure in that inheritance. You can leave pennies on the dollar to your heirs instead of leaving dollars for dollars. It's an effective strategy that the MEC can serve and there's a lot of other uses and tools, but I would argue that is a significant value to be able to have to help hopefully boost retirement income choices have more choices.

Having life insurance gives you the ability to make different choices than you would if didn't have life insurance. Look at any widow who's living well and one who's living poor. The difference usually is how much life insurance was on their spouse before they passed away.

One last thing. Sometimes, whether it's a MEC or a different type of life insurance, the strategies are too good to be true because there is always some form of qualification in the process known as underwriting. This is performed by the company to determine if they can make you an offer for this coverage. This is why it is crucial to be proactive when evaluating its use. I cannot tell you how many times someone neglected or procrastinated on going through the underwriting process and then had a serious medical event. Many times, it is too late to do something after that happens. Companies underwrite differently and it depends on the health event. There may still be options. Do not get discouraged if you feel like your health may disqualify you. There are also guaranteed issue products available so there are other options.

Bonus Number Three

(Long-term care/Life Insurance Hybrids with guaranteed return of premium and no premium increases)

I want to share with you how you can use something called a *combined benefits product* to help your retirement.

It's very simple. People know they need to plan for long-term care. The question is, should you buy a long-term care insurance policy to do that, or should you try to self-insure by building up your own assets? That's something that you're going to have to determine with your advisor.

Some people need life insurance in their portfolio either to settle their estate equitably, to make sure they protect the spouse or a family member, or to use money to transfer your wealth to the next generation.

A combined benefits product is basically those two products put together. You can get life insurance that has a long-term care benefit. If you get sick and need money for care, and you qualify under a care event specified in your policy, the policy will pay out tax-free. Combined benefits products can be extremely valuable to help you to mitigate that risk and expense.

Some of them have true long-term care benefits and some of them are just life insurance benefits that pay out upon death. These products also have what's called an accelerated benefit rider or long-term care rider which allows it to pay out while you're alive if you have a chronic, critical, terminal illness or other care events.

Having a proper blend of two different products can be useful because there may be different waiting periods on products. You may need to have money saved to pay expenses that may later be reimbursed. So, again a combined benefits product could be a great solution to help you offset some of these risks in retirement for pennies on the dollar. Many of these products come with contractual guarantees. Again, there is 100% certainty that no one is making it out of this alive.

There's a 72% chance that if you're married and over the age of 65, one of you will need some form of care. The percentages are extremely high that somebody's going to either need care or pass away, so a combined benefit product will meet the needs of that client 72% of the time or eventually 100% of the time.

Bonus Number Four

(The hidden, most efficient life insurance structure that I've ever created. Plus, a ridiculous story on how you can use this to refinance most debts to work for you rather than against you.)

This may be somewhat difficult to understand unless you are a life insurance agent. However, you can share this section with your agent, and my bet is they'll say, "Wow, I never thought of it like that." So, here we go. When you structure life insurance to build a cash value, if the goal is to access the money potentially tax-free via a policy loan one day as described in bonus number one, then you want to decrease your death benefit to be as low as it can before it's considered a MEC. There are two reasons for that. One, in the MEC, if you fund the policy above that threshold allowed in relation to how much life insurance death benefit you purchase with the policy, the IRS revokes your tax-free loan status. Remember, the IRS absolutely cares how much money you put into these policies in relation to the death benefit.

In the 1980's, the IRS discovered people were cramming large sums of money into whole life insurance. So, they passed these three pieces of legislation:

1. The Tax Equity and Fiscal Responsibility Act (TEFRA) of 1982

2. The Deficit Reduction Act (DEFRA) of 1984

3. The Technical and Miscellaneous Revenue Act (TAMRA) of 1988

These lay the foundation that describe the metrics for what I am discussing above.

*Guideline Premium Test, 7702 Qualification, Cash Value Accumulation Test, Corridor Test, 7-Pay, and Modified Endowment Contract (MEC) These also apply to the combined benefits products.

This can be so much more technical, but it's unnecessary for this book. However, to be accurate, the true most efficient life insurance structure is found in policies still in force that were written prior to this legislation. The second most efficient life insurance structure that may be set up now, is described below.

The second reason an MEC is a more efficient cash value structure is because the goal in building cash value is to reduce internal expenses. Many of the expenses are based on the difference between the death benefit and the cash value. The lower you can get the death benefit to the cash value, the lower you can get the expenses and the cash value can potentially accumulate faster. However, you forfeit your tax-free loan privileges. So, the logical conclusion is that the MEC allows for a smaller death benefit but no tax-free access to cash value policy loans, so then why is that the most efficient?

WARNING: This section contains many industry-specific terms.

Well it's not. Unless you do this: Most of the time, the most effective cash value design is to fund a policy to the max seven-pay premium that you can, then if the policy does not apply, surrender charges. This reduces the face amount to the lowest possible amount that the life insurance company will allow. Then, you can do a 1035 exchange into a new design that is intentionally structured as a MEC with an even lower face amount.

Here is the magic: Once the policy passes through the seven-pay test, it can become a MEC and provide for the tax-free policy loan potential. So, you get the lowest death benefit structure, lowest expenses, and you get the tax-free loan potential! I know this works because I've done it for myself. MECs have other taxable provisions and all solutions should be carefully considered and verified before implementation.

It is also important to note that there really is no such thing as the best. Each solution should be specifically aligned with your individual goals. If your goal is to get the most death benefit to get the highest accelerated death benefit, then you would almost do the opposite structure and none of this cash value design matters. The real word, as Tom Hegna made famous, is optimal. The most optimal means it's going to be right for that circumstance because it will be right more times than it is wrong and is better than the other options. These are not to be considered accurate representations of these complex tax laws. These are also not recommendations directly for you. Again, in case you're not sick of this yet, this is not tax or investment advice. You need to consult with the right professional who is licensed and proficient in this method before acting on anything described in this book. I also strongly encourage everyone who is serious about building these strategies to read "Look Before You LIRP" by David McKight. I know, I know – another book.

These strategies are meant to be with you until you take your last breath, and in some cases until your children's entire lives, and grandchildren's, etc. This is potentially generational wealth. If you can't read a book or two and meet with a life insurance agent a few times, then I don't know what to tell you other than, "It deserves a few hours of your attention because it could be the difference between the retirement you always talked about and a much different reality at your most vulnerable place in life." Simply put, it's the difference between freedom and regret. Please put in the time and work with the right professional. Now, back to the nifty fun creative stuff that YOU can do now.

Here is an example similar to this structure, but an incredible way the end result can solve so many problems for retirees and pre-retires today!

A common problem I see amongst families is one family member loans money to another family member and now they're stuck with this loan. Maybe they're making payments on it. Maybe they are slow paying it, but there's a more efficient way you can structure this amongst your family.

Recently, a lady came into my office and told me her daughter had borrowed money to refinance some high-interest credit card debt. Then, the daughter hit on some hard financial times.

She was slow paying her mom and not quite making monthly payments each month. Not only was she not able to refinance all the debt, the mom was actually still a co-signer on part of the high-interest debt and the daughter was barely making the minimum payment. There was never going to be a scenario where they'd pay off all the debt. So in the meantime, the mom's out money because she loaned the daughter money to help refinance some of the debt. The daughter's slowly paying her back. The mom's still on part of the other loan, which is at high interest and impacting her credit and her ability to borrow. And the daughter's nowhere near paying these things off. So, what do you do? Right? You have a high-interest scenario. The mom's out money, the daughters out money, then nobody's happy. So, I told her about something I call a secured loan alternative. Now that is not the proper term for the strategy because there is no term for the strategy. I've never found one. I've used this for many, many years for myself.

The mom tells me about her savings account, which is barely earning anything. She has well beyond her liquid needs and she's got a surplus of money that's sitting in an online money market earning 2%.

At the same time, this mom also has a need for some potential life insurance and she may experience a care event at some point in her retirement where she would need money to help take care of her if she became permanently disabled. So again, I'm painting a picture here because there's a solution that nobody's considering.

Very complex scenario, right? But a fun problem to solve. So enter in a fun scenario that I like to draw up using a participating loan feature from life insurance. When you have a participating loan feature, you can use your money for whatever you need it for, but it's going to participate in the interest that the policy can potentially earn.

There is an interest cost going against the money you loan out. For example, let's say you have $100,000 in the life insurance policy and you pull out $50,000. There's a 4% interest rate assessed against the $50,000 and then anything you potentially earn in interest or dividends can credit to your policy after you pay the 4%. So you can loan your money out, use it, and potentially earn interest on it while it's the policy still thinks it's in there.

Let me say that another way. You can essentially borrow your money out and instead of losing the interest-earning potential, Pretty cool strategy, right? How can you do this? Well, because there's a big death benefit on the backend of the policy that states if you never pay back that loan to yourself, the insurance company will subtract it from your death benefit, the loan plus the interest and pay your beneficiary the difference.

Here's where this gets kind of creative and exciting. We set up a life insurance policy on mom. Mom puts $50,000 in the policy right away, which creates a modified endowment contract. Which means that her earnings are no longer going to be potentially tax-free in the form of a loan. The earnings are tax-deferred still but taxable based on her ordinary income at the time of the loan or withdrawal. Her interest was taxable in the money market any-way. When we set up this modified endowment contract, it came with $120,000 worth of life insurance and $120,000 will also pay out if mom gets sick and needs money for care, thereby addressing two of her needs. To structure the life insurance so she was not required to pay an annual premium, we also had to structure some benefit that would pay out for care without paying premiums out of her income for long-term care insurance.

Her $50,000 goes into the policy and it has the potential to earn interest up and above the savings account. There's three needs taken care of, but here's where it gets crazy. She can take a $40,000 loan from that policy to pay off the daughter's two loans. That costs mom 4% to get the money out. Mom takes a 4% loan to pay off the daughter's two loans. This wipes out the one high-interest loan and the other loan that she made to her daughter, but the daughter is still responsible for making payments to her mom. Now here's where it gets exciting. Mom's being charged for the loan from the life insurance company, but she's not charging interest to her daughter. Her daughter's previous loan had an interest rate of 18%. So, as a daughter makes the payments back to mom, a couple of things happen.

One, mom's still earning money on the policy for the money that's loaned out. The $40,000 is loaned out to pay off those two lenders. It's now gone from the policy, but she's still able to potentially earn higher interest on it than she could in the savings account. And I say potential as it's not guaranteed that she would do that, but she may be able to. Remember, Mom is now no longer paying 18% interest and damaging her credit score. Instead, she's making the potential interest in the policy plus she has life insurance and a care benefit, not long-term care insurance, but a potential care benefit associated with an accelerated death benefit with the policy for a potential care event that could occur.

So, a lot of her needs are met. She's off the hook for that high-interest loan. The loan from her policy is not negatively impacting her credit score.

Now, let's say daughter's still on hard financial times. She has been slow paying mom, she's paying month-to-month. Some months she can pay a little. Some months she can pay more. Well, the previous lender doesn't care if daughter's on hard times or not. There's an amortization schedule with that loan. If she doesn't make that payments, they're going to default. She'll default on it and they're going to foreclose on her and there's going to be repercussions. That could also have potentially negative tax impacts to the mom and daughter.

Mom could be sued by that lender if the daughter can't make the payments, but what happens with the life insurance policy if the daughter can't make the payments and never pays her back at all? That $40,000 is gone. What happens to life insurance policy? Well, because we've structured it so effectively, the cash value of $10,000 left in mom's policy that she didn't loan out could potentially grow back to $50,000, and over time, if daughter never paid a dime back to the policy, not only could it grow back to $50,000 but the death benefit and benefit that we're paying for care could continue to grow as well. And you say, "Wow, what a crazy idea on how to structure all these strategies to be met for this one scenario, using a conventional process I call a secured loan alternative through life insurance."

I call it a secured loan alternative because you can go to a credit union or bank. Most of the time, mom could put that $50,000 down, create a secured loan against that asset and borrow money at 4%. Why would she do that, when she could put it in a life insurance policy and get the other benefits associated with it? If the daughter never paid back the money, it could potentially grow back on its own because of that participating loan feature.

There are a lot of scenarios. There may be a person who has one or two of those needs, maybe not all of them. This is where the value of life insurance can come into play. It's one dollar doing the job of many dollars. You see that the $50,000 she deposits in the policy-provided life insurance, a care benefit, offers relief from liabilities such as default remedies and a negatively impacted credit score, less family tension, an automatic repayment of the debt by recapturing the daughter's inheritance with her portion of the death benefit of the policy going to repay any unpaid loan balance.

So again, it provides many, many benefits, and I wanted to bring that up because not many people would think to use it in that capacity, but it has as you can see it has a place here.

Disclaimers

Publication 525 is how I read it and is my interpretation. Pub 525 deals with a wide verity of taxable and no taxable incomes and is not solely focused on the paragraphs I am referring to.

For more detailed analysis of long-term care, you should consult with a licensed long-term care health insurance agent.

It's not easy to find this information. I wrote the book I wanted to read myself.

It may be an option to help you and your loved ones have at a quality retirement. We owe it to future generations by living in this era of borrowing from their future reflected in our national debt, to at least share quality strategies like this with them. I plan to take this on the road. Creating local presentations across the United States with a select group of specially trained like-minded agents in cities everywhere, but please don't wait. Get this book in the hands of the people you love. Please don't keep it a secret. My life's work only means something if I get to share it with action takers like yourself.

Sincerely, from the bottom of my heart, thank you, and God Bless.

Sources

Bankrate.com

USDebtClock.org

IRAHelp.com

CBO.org

SkilledNursing.org

LongTermCare.org

Medicare.gov

JeffBushSpeaks.com

Trieste.gov

HealthViewServices.com

IRS.gov

BureauofLaborStatistics.com

Finviz.com

LaurenceKotlikoff.com

TomHegna.com

VanMueller.com

Power of Zero

Look Before you LIRP Retirement

Retirement Alpha

Pay Checks and Play Checks

Don't Worry, Retire Happy!

Social Security and Medicare Trustees

Report Center for Tax Awareness

Forbes

The Wall Street Journal

Boston Research Corporation

Investopedia

MarketWatch

Milliman Health Index

US Census Bureau

Taxcaster
AARP
A-Z Quotes
Brainy Quotes
Good Reads
Wikipedia
Four Hour Work Week
Unshakable
Tax Foundation
Charles Schwab
Fidelity
Edward Jones
J.P. Morgan
Merrill Lynch
Tax Cuts and Jobs Act 2017
TaxPolicyCenter.org
FightChronicDisease.org

About the Author

Daniel Rondberg - The Retirement Specialist

Daniel Rondberg Nation's First Financial Retirement Specialist
The Retirement Research Foundation Course Educator

Daniel Rondberg is a retirement authority. He's spoken to and taught financial professionals and consumers all over the country. His mission is simple: reach as many pre-retirees as soon as possible to help them enjoy the best years of their lives!

Daniel Rondberg began his career working at JP Morgan, but later felt drawn to embrace the family business and went on to become an independent retirement specialist at Nation's First Financial in their Mesa, Arizona office. Daniel's success has been quick and consistent. The value he provides is demonstrated to his clients through his focus on tax reduction and retirement security, although his greatest strength is listening and honoring his clients' concerns by customizing solutions that align with their core beliefs. In addition, he teaches educational workshops on retirement and is a published author in a well-known industry trade publication furnished by Ideal Producers Group. In 2016,

2017, 2018, and 2019 he was recognized as the number one life specialist by the same company.

Daniel enjoys helping people breathe easy when it comes to retirement and traveling with his family. He lives in Mesa, Arizona with his lovely wife, Jennifer, and his daughters Cassidy and Spencer. Together they are dedicated to traveling the world and sharing their message.

- National Speaker

- Published Author

- Creator of the Life Hacks Unlimited Life Program

- Oversees more than 100 million in client's retirement assets and Life Insurance Benefits

My personal site: https://www.DanielRondberg.com

My Vlog: https://www.RetirementByDanielRondberg.com

My FREE Social Security Maximization Webinar:
http://www.retire-mentresearchfoundation.org/social-security-maximization-webinar

My Agency's site: https://www.NationsFirstFin.com

My Industry Insider's podcast:
https://RealWealthMedia.com/Danny-Rondberg

My YouTube Channel
https://www.YouTube.com/channel/UC52cim- 6wfLu7WqnlyJtfUxQ

My podcast: http://www.BuzzSprout.com/695890

Financial Professionals: Please check out Daniel's course which can be found on Teachable that outlines how to set up the strategies described in this book.

Made in the USA
Coppell, TX
19 November 2020